The A-Z of Ministry with Children
Erratum: Table of Contents

All page numbers listed are in error by 2
e.g. 7 should be 5; 9 should be 7 and so on

Acknowledgments

This book springs from one that was published under the same title in 1992. While some sections are identical, the earlier book has been comprehensibly revised and expanded into two. *The A-Z of Ministry with Children* concentrates on very practical aspects of ministry with children and *The A-Z of Presenting Christian Concepts* will outline tried and tested ways of explaining Bible truths in ways that make sense to children.

In this respect I had the assistance of Andrew Cupples, from the publishing staff of Scripture Union England and Wales. Andrew worked through the earlier book, dividing it up and making comments. His expertise is warmly appreciated. I commend Ivan Smith of Communique Graphics for his imaginative flair with all aspects of design and Sally Smith too for considerable time and effort spent in taking the project to completion.

Most of the contents of this book are the work of Michael Perini and myself. Michael lectures with me in Christian Education at the Sydney Missionary and Bible College. He was previously a school chaplain at Barker College and more recently has had considerable input in the area of teacher training, as well as being in demand as a speaker at school assemblies.

A number of fellow children's workers have also been involved. Graham Wade contributed in the area of technology, particularly the sections on DVD/Video clips and Video-Making. Readers will value the detailed notes and diagrams of Kathy Sloss, a long-time teacher of Special Religious Education, for illustrating a teaching session. Margaret Layson, an expert in calligraphy, has given valuable insights to improve publicity through thoughtful use of colour and design. Trevor Muddle, who has extensive experience in teaching severely disabled children, graciously accepted our invitation to write a section for those involved with children with intellectual disabilities.

In the after-school missions that I conducted for a number of years, no tool proved more valuable in capturing and maintaining the interest of children than a well-produced puppet drama. Rob French, who recently rebuilt my puppet theatre, has added the section on puppetry. Leanne Palmer, children's ministry specialist and former SU staff worker, has written to inform readers about working with pre-adolescents. Our thanks too, to Lionel Dickinson who supplied many extra illustrations. We are thankful for each of these people who have so willingly shared their expertise.

My hope is that with the benefit of input from all these people, this new edition will prove even more beneficial than the last.

Owen Shelley

introduction

In the era of the gold rushes, some miners tapped into rich seams and made fortunes, while others went away empty-handed.

As the miners dug for the elusive nuggets, they threw up large mullock heaps of clay and gravel. When a field was considered to be 'worked out', the miners moved on, to be replaced by fossickers who sifted through the mullock heaps, often finding gold that the miners had missed. Even today, there are visitors to the old goldfields who, armed with metal detectors, shovels and sieves, hope to strike it rich.

The original *A to Z of Ministry with Children* was like a gold mine. There were some very productive seams – such as sketching – that proved valuable to all who were persuaded to start digging there. For this book, Owen has thoroughly re-worked his original material. Where there were gaps, others have been invited to add their specialties.

Each of us who are contributors want to say that there are some time-tested and proven nuggets to be discovered which can be deposited in your bank of kids' ministry ideas. If you have already worked in the mine of the first edition, let us suggest that there is, in this revision, sufficient gold available for fossickers to take up shovels again and start sieving.

For all of you, old hands and new prospectors alike, we trust that the ideas and know-how expressed here will help to make your work with children more productive.

May the children know, through who you are and what you teach, that Jesus is the Way and his Father is the Destination.

Michael Perini

contents

Topic...*Page*

Abstract ideas ... 7
Advertising ... 9
After-school events ... 11
Aims ... 12
Analogy ... 15
Artwork ... 16
Beginning a children's talk ... 18
Bible readings ... 20
Books for children's workers ... 21
Bubble writing ... 23
Classroom management ... 24
Colour ... 26
Conclusions ... 28
Control and discipline ... 29
Copyright ... 33
Craft ... 34
Design ... 36
Dialogue ... 38
Drama ... 41
DVD / Video Clips ... 43
Easels ... 44
Embellishment ... 46
Enthusiasm ... 48
Eye contact ... 49
Finding a new angle ... 50
First person recital ... 52
Flashcard pictures ... 54
Flexibility ... 57
Games ... 58
Helping children to trust Jesus ... 63
Holiday Bible clubs ... 65
Icebreakers ... 69
Illustrating a story ... 70
'Inbetweeners' (10 to 13-year-olds) ... 83
Intellectually handicapped children ... 87
Inviting a response ... 88
Jesus ... 90

Topic...*Page*

Language barriers ... 92
Legibility ... 94
Links in storytelling ... 96
Memorising Bible verses ... 97
Metaphors ... 100
Names ... 101
Opening the Bible with children ... 102
Overhead projectors ... 104
Participation ... 107
Planning/ preparation ... 108
Prayer ... 109
Problems ... 110
Project-o-graph ... 111
Publicity ... 113
Puppetry ... 115
Quick sketching ... 121
Quiz games ... 127
Relationships ... 130
Researching Bible stories ... 131
Revision ... 134
School assemblies ... 135
Script writing ... 137
Serial stories ... 139
Singing ... 140
Storytelling ... 142
Tempo ... 146
Understanding children ... 147
Venues ... 149
Video-making ... 150
Visi-wheel story ... 151
Visual aids ... 155
Voice ... 157
Wonder wall ... 158
Words ... 159
Writing ... 160
Zest ... 160

abstract ideas

Children are concrete thinkers. They are still developing the ability to think in abstract terms. The difficulty in sharing biblical concepts with them, is that 'grace', 'forgiveness', 'faith', 'trust', and 'salvation' are all abstract concepts. The challenge for teachers and children's speakers is to take these abstract concepts and express them in concrete terms so children can understand them.

Ron Buckland in *Children and the Gospel* says that an abstract concept is one that can't be drawn. You can't show or draw a 'grace', although you can speak of a king who showed grace to his subjects. You can't draw a 'forgiveness', although you can draw a picture of a girl kissing a boy when she forgives him for being late. You can describe the actions of people who demonstrate faith but you cannot describe 'faith' without using other abstract words like 'confidence' or 'trust'.

Stephanie Carmichael in *Their God is so Big*, uses the way maths is taught in school to illustrate the point. Young children learn to count by playing with objects, then they progress to the symbols written on paper.

Concrete	children picking up and handling 4 then 3 blocks.
Less concrete	a drawing of 4 red blocks and 3 blue blocks making 7 blocks.
Abstract	4+3=7 (arithmetic)
The very abstract	a+b=c (algebra)

Stories

Sometimes we can't avoid speaking abstractly but we need to be aware when we are doing so, and not overdo it. One of the best ways to explain an abstract concept is to put it into a story. The story makes the concept concrete and reveals the abstract. For example, in Luke 15 Jesus teaches that 'lostness' implies that something or someone is valued. The shepherd valued the lost sheep. The widow valued the lost coin. The father valued the lost son. People who have lost contact with God are valued.

Watch out for stories in everyday life, books and the media that can be used to teach or reveal an abstract concept. Children's movies often contain examples. For example in ***Finding Nemo****, Marlin risks his life many times to find and save his son. Referring to that story can help children understand the concept of sacrifice. Become an obsessive collector of these stories and use them!*

Symbols – the door illustration

In Scripture there are not only abstract terms such as 'grace' and 'faith,' but abstract symbols as well.

Take the example in John 10 where Jesus uses the symbol of a gate or doorway to describe himself and his purpose.

> What is a doorway? It's a space in a wall that enables us to go from one room into another. We do not usually climb through a window unless we lose our keys!
>
> A door may be marked 'storeroom'. We go through that doorway if we want to find something we expect to be stored there. Another door may be marked 'Principal'. When we go through that doorway we expect to meet the Principal of the school. The door gives us access to the Principal's presence.
>
> When Jesus said, 'I am the door', he didn't mean that he was a hole in the wall or that he was made of wood. He meant that through him we could come to know God and belong to him.

This example moves from the concrete to the abstract in gradual steps. This is a hazardous journey at any time, and requires careful thought, but it is essential if we are going to succeed in explaining abstract ideas to children.

advertising

See also ***Colour, Design, Publicity***

There's no doubt, it pays to advertise.

Leaflets are the most common advertising tool. They should state clearly whom you represent. It's wise to indicate a finishing as well as the starting time for activities. Whatever you promise on your leaflet, make sure you deliver.

Think creatively

'Boys and Girls, ask inside for your free pass to the What-cha-ma-call-it show', said notices in the shopwindows.

Local shopkeepers had been persuaded to display the signs and become unpaid distribution agents for tickets to an after-school programme at the church. The tickets gave the details of the time and place, but also read 'Admit Two', the idea being that some children are too shy to ask for themselves.

Investigate banners, posters, leaflets, colouring competitions and ads in local papers and on local radio. One church centre hired a helium-filled navigation balloon which they flew each day before their holiday club.

At Toowoon Bay, where the beach mission team was celebrating its fortieth summer, the team borrowed an elephant from a local circus, and every person in their camping area turned out to see it. It's surprising what you can achieve when you ask!

Make the programme extra appealing

The best advertisement is always the programme itself. Many five-day holiday clubs have small numbers on the first day but numbers build as the word spreads. Some that have been running for years have a long waiting list. If this is not the case, it's worth examining the programme to see if it's appealing.

> A young theological student had been asked to take over the running of the Sunday children's group at the church where he had been appointed as an assistant. In the past, the enrolment had reportedly been in the vicinity of three hundred but now only fifteen attended.
>
> 'What should I do to promote the Sunday school? Should I organise a visitation programme or prepare a letterbox drop?'

He was advised that his first step should be to make the programme so appealing that the 'fifteen' couldn't wait to get there each week. A few months later, he reported that attendances had doubled.

The name you give your club or event can add to its appeal.

In a talk at a children's camp, a Christian was defined as someone who *Believes, Behaves* and *Belongs*. On returning home to the little township of Tambar Springs, an after-school club was started with the telling name of *The 3B Club*.

after-school events

See also ***Control and Discipline***

Whether you are conducting an after-school mission or a once a week kids' club, after-school events have common characteristics and there are some things you need to do.

The children may have been regimented for most of the day and need to be allowed to let off steam. Some active games can be useful at this point.

The team members who are marshalling the children should

- Show them where to leave their bags
- Show them where to enrol and/or have their attendance marked
- Encourage them to make a toilet stop (Failure to give this reminder can cause havoc later because, when one child asks to go, others will want to follow.)
- Indicate where they should line up for a snack

When it's time to move indoors, it can be helpful to ask them to line up at the door. Bring the younger children to the head of the line and allow them in first so that they will be seated at the front. Keep control at this point and prevent pushing and shoving. This pays dividends in later control in the session.

Some kids' clubs conduct their together times in the church because it allows them to have the church hall set up ready for messy activities such as craft and refreshments. If the together time is not part of a programme of this type, the hall will prove to be the better location for the meeting, especially if the church has fixed pews with high backs which make control more difficult.

The most important task in the preparation of a children's programme or talk is to define clearly your aim.

The aim isn't to teach geography

There may be some geographical information in your teaching but your primary purpose isn't to familiarise your pupils with the geography of the Holy Land, the way things were in Bible times, or the sequence of places visited by Paul on his missionary journeys. These issues are incidental.

The aim isn't to teach history

Our teaching is based upon historical events so we will be eager to show that we are not merely telling myths and legends which have no historical basis. Nevertheless, if we only succeed in communicating who did what and where and when, we will have failed to achieve our basic purpose. Biblical knowledge has little value if taught for its own sake.

The aim isn't to teach morality

While it can be shown that our Christian teaching has a strong moral purpose, this cannot be the main aim of our message because we recognise that striving to live a good life is always insufficient to win our salvation. No matter how hard we try, we still fall short.

If our primary purpose isn't to teach history, geography or morality, what is it?

The general aim of children's ministry

1 Corinthians 15:3 states

> *What I received I passed on to you as of first importance: that Christ died for our sins according to the Scriptures, that he was buried, that he was raised on the third day...*

If we were to attempt to sum up our message in one word, it would surely be 'Jesus'. In a short-term project such as a holiday club, which occurs only once a year, it's a good plan to stick to the reported incidents of Jesus' life. In functions such as a weekly kids' club, our range of topics and stories will be much wider, though still keeping in mind that we want the children to know Jesus.

The specific aim of a session

The aim you choose will, of course, depend on the children in your particular group. How much do they already know and practise? Are they from unchurched families? Are they part of your church? If you are a visitor, ask as many questions as possible about the group you will be addressing. How many children are in the group? What are their ages? Are they regulars at the club? Answering these questions enables you to decide where to place the emphasis. If you work regularly with a group, you should have a greater understanding of their needs, but be on guard lest you lose sight of your general aim and lapse into teaching geography, history or morality. Choose *one* clear teaching point for your talk, then plan your talk to communicate that teaching point. Resist the temptation to make additional points. If you teach from a prepared syllabus, recognise that it is easy for lesson book compilers to fall into the same trap.

Select a single aim

Whether you are dealing with children or adults, a single aim is likely to be more successful. It is helpful to write the aim of your message down in one simple sentence. If you cannot do so, you are attempting to achieve too much.

In researching your biblical material, you may find that several important and legitimate messages emerge from the story. They all may belong there and all may be attractive to you as themes to explore in your talk. Having studied the story, you may have no trouble in keeping all the themes clear in your head but the poor audience does not know what is coming and can be easily confused. Confusion is as big a barrier to your message as boredom!

So, choose your particular aim. Select the major theme or lesson that emerges from the biblical narrative, then craft the talk around it, carefully working all the material so that the message emerges clearly.

For example, if you wanted to use the story of Jacob and Esau in Genesis 25 and 32 for older audiences, you might decide to explore the biblical doctrine of propitiation. After describing Jacob's deceit and Esau's violent threats, move quickly to the account of Jacob's return home twenty years later (Genesis 32), skipping over all the information relating to Jacob contained in chapters 26–31 as this is not relevant to your purpose on this occasion. Place your emphasis on Jacob's intention to pacify his brother's anger with an elaborate gift (Genesis 32:29).

With a younger audience, however, you might wish to use the same story to illustrate the more straightforward theme of reconciliation. You could begin with a lively story of a child

having a disagreement with a friend, and lead on to describe that the brothers became friends again.

Make your teaching relevant

Have you ever heard someone address a group of children and use such examples as exceeding the speed limit or cheating on a tax return? If what we say to children is irrelevant to their experience of life, then our stories and illustrations will confuse rather than enhance our teaching.

> A group of teachers was discussing the previous week's lesson. As suggested in their teaching manual, they had each used a bottle of sand to illustrate the promise made to Abraham that his descendants would be as numerous as the grains of sand on the beach. When the teachers later questioned their classes about the lesson they drew a blank on that part of their lesson. The children remembered that Abraham had been promised extensive land holdings, but they did not recall the promise relating to numerous descendants. This was puzzling. It seems that the answer lay in the fact that, the prospect of Abraham becoming 'the father of many nations' held little significance for children.

Ensuring that our teaching is relevant is an ongoing struggle. To stay in tune with the world of today's boys and girls is a very valuable skill which you can't get from books. Grasp opportunities when they present themselves to chat to children.

Correctly handle the Word of Truth

Study the story in its context. What happens before and after the event can give insight into its significance. It's also useful to examine all the accounts of an event as this may give fuller details. Resist the temptation to use the Bible simply to support your own ideas or to fit a clever talk outline.

By 'analogy' we mean telling one story under the disguise of another.

Last century there was a common tendency among children's speakers to turn Bible stories into analogies. For example, using Jesus' story of the Good Samaritan and the letters A, L and S, the injured man on the roadway is referred to as 'a lost sinner', the Samaritan as 'a loving saviour', and, the rescued man became 'a live saint'.

The problem with this approach is that when Jesus told the story he did it to teach who our neighbour is, and the above outline ignores that fact. When a Bible story is converted to an analogy, the story's central truth changes. You will know you are switching to analogy when you use the phrase 'This is like…'

Some speakers turn Bible stories into analogies in order to increase the amount of salvation theology. They do this either when they are anxious to impress their hearers with the importance of making an immediate response to their teaching, or to show that a Bible story is relevant to their lives. Such 'analogising' can also lead us to interpret Bible stories in quite fanciful ways. The parable of the Good Samaritan again comes to mind as an example; the following dialogue is from a play based on that parable.

Innkeeper: You've done a wonderful thing. Why did you stop to help him when others walked past?

Samaritan: I'm a Christian and I read my Bible every day and it teaches me to help others.

Innkeeper: If reading the Bible did that for you, I'd better begin to read my Bible too.

Clearly, the writer of this play wanted to drive home the importance of Bible reading, and hoped that the audience would be eager to go home and begin this good habit. Unfortunately this application ignores the parable's central message, which is to answer the question 'who is my neighbour?' It demonstrates a lack of submission to the Bible as the Word of God.

It can be said in general that attempting to teach Christian truths by teaching something different will fail to teach the truth, unless you risk both boredom and confusion by explaining all the connections between the analogy and the truth.

artwork

There are many books and copyright-free sources of visuals to enhance your presentations. Photocopiers and computers can enlarge and reduce at will, and clip art can be stored and manipulated in your own computer. Have fun exploring these options.

Styles of art change and it is important not to downgrade your ministry by associating it with art that your audience considers is out of fashion.

Artwork that illustrates a book of Bible stories is entirely different from that which is best for a class or assembly. In the latter situation, the pictures should aim for clarity of impact by avoiding too much detail. To test a picture's suitability, display it, then view it from the positions of those who will be closest and farthest away. If the picture is meaningless for either, then it is not suitable.

Be true to the times

A series of pictures illustrating the Bible story of the journey of the twelve spies in Numbers 13, showed some spies hiding in a ditch, dressed in Akubra hats and peering through binoculars. Clearly, the artist thought this would be amusing, but there is a problem with such amusement. The drawing was not true to the historical period in which it occurred, and could convey the idea that the Bible is book of funny stories and jokes.

Reveal the emotions

Those who have produced clip art for our benefit are to be warmly commended. Where would we be without such valuable tools as *How to Cheat at Visual Aids* published by Scripture Union? Some clip art is, however, emotionally bland, and while depicting actions, does nothing to convey feelings. Good illustration helps to convey emotion, as shown in this illustration of the panic caused when the Midianites invaded Israel in Gideon's day.

If we compare the normal run of biblical artwork with that in action comics, biblical art is decidedly tame. Admittedly, action comics are extreme, and we are not advocating that we copy them, but we do want to convey emotions as realistically as possible. After all, the people we are illustrating really lived lives that were as full of emotion as our own.

beginning a children's talk

If you want to be an effective communicator of God's good news, there's no point starting tentatively. Arrest attention from the beginning.

If you could X-ray the minds of your audience, you would find they wander many pathways! To prevent this, appeal to their curiosity. Here are several ways to do this:

A question

Direct questions are those which expect an answer: 'If you saw a man with a white walking stick what would you know about him?' Rhetorical questions require no answer: 'If you saw a man with a white walking stick, you would know he was blind, wouldn't you?' Either question could lead into the story of blind Bartimaeus. (Be careful with rhetorical questions because younger children will often try to give you an answer.)

Questions arouse the curiosity of your audience. 'I've got something in my pocket that is alive. What do you think it is?' (Taking out a seed can introduce a lesson on the parable of the sower.)

A brief story about another child (or children)

This can either be true or imagined. Tell your audience which it is. If it is true, be careful not to exaggerate. Here's an example.

> Bill had a new tennis racquet and was enjoying hitting a ball against the wall of his house. 'Bill, don't play there, you might break the window!' warned his mother. Despite her warning, Bill continued to play until...smash, tinkle, tinkle...the ball went straight through the glass. Dropping the racquet, Bill ran and hid up a tree in the paddock down the road. Later, when it began to grow dark, he slowly made his way home, very upset. When his mother saw his distress, she comforted him instead of punishing him.

(This introduction could lead into a talk about separation and reconciliation.)

Something topical

Here's an example of a topical start to a talk. It could lead to a talk on the concept of propitiation, using 1 Samuel 25, Abigail seeking to pacify David's anger.

> Who saw the television programme about volcanoes on *The World Around Us?* It showed people in Hawaii throwing fruit and vegetables into a volcano. They thought the mountain was a god and that the mountain must be angry with them because he was about to erupt. They were giving their god a gift to make him happy.

Start well into a Bible story

When planning to recount a Bible story, work out the best place to begin. The best start is often not the beginning of the story but towards the end, in fact, as close to the end as possible. Sounds strange? Look at the following example.

> Goliath the giant muttered to himself as he strapped on his heavy helmet and picked up his enormous spear. 'This is becoming ridiculous!' he grumbled. 'Every day for the past month I've been challenging these chicken-hearted Israelites to send a champion to fight me. It's a waste of breath.'
>
> The Philistine champion lumbered over to the edge of the valley and, after taking a deep breath, began to shout. 'Hey! Over there! Send out someone to fight me. If he can beat me, we will be your servants, but if I beat him, then… What? Don't tell me someone is coming! I don't believe it!'

This introduction has the following features

- It introduces the antagonist (the hero's opponent) early, so that we know what the protagonist (the hero) is up against. This is an important technique in building suspense.
- It plunges into the action – the moment of combat is only moments away. The effect is more gripping than starting by describing David making his way to the battle front.
- It uses a good deal of dialogue, which has a fascination for the listeners.
- It uses colourful language like 'muttered', 'grumbled', 'lumbered'.
- It uses an interrupted line or a pause: 'If I beat him, then…'

Actively involve the children

Another method of getting started is to use a series of questions aimed at involving your whole group. For example, for a lesson to explain faith, based on the raising of Jairus' daughter, ask 'What is the opposite of fat (thin), short (tall), rich (poor), love (hate), faith (doubt)?' You may discover that 'doubt' is not a term that all are familiar with, so give a brief explanation. Then continue by explaining that while Jairus demonstrated faith when he came to Jesus to ask for healing for his daughter, his faith must have wavered when messengers reported her death. Recognising his doubt, Jesus hastened to reassure him (Luke 8:50).

bible readings

It's difficult to hold the attention of children with a plain Bible reading. Alert the children beforehand to a question you intend to ask when the reading is over, so they have a reason for listening.

To capture audience attention, a Bible reading in which a different reader takes the part of each character is better than one reader. Using visuals such an overhead projector with overlay figures or a PowerPoint® presentation is another option. Such visuals should be operated by an assistant, not the reader.

In ministering to adults, it is common to read the Bible before explaining it. This is not a good practice with children. If you read the Bible story before you tell it, the children will know how it ends, and lose interest.

On the other hand, reading the Bible account of Jonah before seeing a puppet play on the same material can increase the children's appreciation of the play which should, in turn, make the Scriptures come alive for them.

At a family service or another function where a reading from the Scripture is the accepted procedure, instead of reading the story on which you intend to speak, select a passage that has a similar emphasis.

If, in situations such as school assemblies, the readers are children, it's important that they practise beforehand. If the passage contains names that they are likely to stumble over, perhaps select a different passage. If a microphone is to be used, make sure that it is adjusted to the reader's height, pointed towards their mouth, and that they are close enough for the voice to be picked up clearly.

books for children's workers

There are many books written about ministry with children.

Sometimes a book contains only one main principle or idea. For that single idea it can be money well spent and shelf space worth giving. By creating a filing system (on cards or computer) you can shorten the searching time and the inevitable disappointment in not being able to find an idea, a quote, an illustration or an explanation.

The books listed can be grouped under two headings:

- **Platform books** give guiding principles on which to build understanding
- **Dive in** books give do-it-yourself ideas.

Platform books

Knowing God (Hodder and Stoughton) and *Concise Theology* (Tyndale House) by JI Packer are two titles which are scholarly, yet easily understood. They explain theological terms and concepts.

Christian Basics (Hodder and Stoughton) and *The Contemporary Christian* (IVP) by John Stott set out the fundamentals of what it means to be a Christian. Both these books have much to say and model ways on how best to say it.

Children Finding Faith (Scripture Union) by Francis Bridger and *Children and the Gospel* (Scripture Union) by Ron Buckland are books that will inform your understanding of children and set out the pertinent theological considerations.

The Very Essential Must-Have Really Useful Guide to Working with Children (Scripture Union) is a useful reference. Although only 36 pages in length, it covers a diverse range of topics, is easily understood and very practical.

Dive in books

In *The Adventure Begins* (Scripture Union), Terry Clutterham shares insights into opening the Bible with children. It includes examples of creative activities so children can discover the Bible in meaningful ways for themselves.

A Storyteller's Guide to the Old Testament and *A Storyteller's Guide to the Gospels* (Scripture Union) are companion books. Owen Shelley highlights action and emotion, vital ingredients in arresting and maintaining the focus of any audience.

Theme Games 1 and *Theme Games 2* (Scripture Union) by Lesley Pinchbeck each have over 100 games arranged thematically. The author's aim is to supply just the right game that links to the teaching programme.

Everyone's a Winner! Over 200 co-operative games for 7-13 year olds (Scripture Union) by Ruth Willis is an illustrated book with a radically different approach to games.

Children's Talks: A Practical Guide (Sydney Missionary Bible College) by Sandy Galea is full of very helpful principles and examples of creative talks ready to be practised and presented.

Their God is So Big (Matthias Media) by Stephanie Carmichael is designed for those working with children up to 8 years. There are principles, practical tips and ideas for delivering arresting Bible-based lessons.

The *Working with* ... series from Scripture Union comes in different books for different ages. Each contains pretty much everything you need to know to equip and inspire you in working with the age group.

KidsWise, an Australian magazine published quarterly by Scripture Union, will keep you up to date with the latest ideas and resources to use in ministry with children. It can be ordered at www.scriptureunion.org.au

bubble writing

Bubble writing gives older children the chance to colour the letters and it's fun to copy.

ABCDEFGH

IJKLMNOP

QRSTUV

WXYZ

classroom management

See also ***Control and Discipline, Names, Relationships***

Being fully prepared is the key to successful, stress-free classroom teaching.

Be prepared

- If you use set lesson material, skim through it a week before you have to teach it. Skim, don't plan in detail. As the days go by, with the lesson in your mind, you are giving your creativity time to surface. Your oral illustrations, visual aids, lesson introductions, fun activities and theological understanding have free time to 'bubble along'.
- Divide the whole lesson into small 'time islands'. They could be Motivation/ Introduction island, Content island, Activity island, End-of-the-Lesson island. Prepare for what will happen as you arrive at each 'island'.
- Check that all equipment is working properly and cued exactly.

Handle disruptions

If you are a visitor in the classroom, find out how the regular teacher handles disruptions and use the same system. A tried and true method of handling any children who are disrupting the lesson is to write their names on the board. You may need to add Xs or underline the name if the disruption continues. The class must know and understand the consequences of not cooperating and you must carry out those consequences if necessary. Have no more than two Xs or underlines before you take action as otherwise your threat will not be taken seriously. In the school situation, the consequence is usually reporting to the school authorities, a step you may be reluctant to take. Sadly, in some situations, this may be necessary. As the offending child's co-operation and focus improves during the lesson, begin to erase the Xs and letters of the name, at the same time commending the child for being co-operative.

Be keen to reward good behaviour and co-operation. Stickers and praising them in front of their peers and/or regular teacher are usually very effective.

Keep the children involved

If you are reading (not telling) a long story without any pictures, allow the class to doodle while you read. Reading is not ideal because you can't maintain eye contact with the class, but the doodling will soon dwindle if the story is interesting and well read.

When you ask a question and you affirm one child's answer, ask 'Who else was going to say that?' Encourage all to be involved in answering by suggesting alternative answers and asking for show-of-hands.

Every child should have something to do at every moment. Have extra activities available for those who finish quickly. Simple puzzle sheets and memory verse jigsaw pieces in plastic sleeves will keep them involved while others finish.

Often the toughest time of the lesson is the last five minutes, particularly if you have finished what you planned. Have several quiet time-fillers ready, such as

- a quick show-of-hands opinion survey (The person I most admire..., The best way to impress people..., Best thing to do on a Saturday, Favourite TV programme...)
- a revision quiz
- 'Who'd like to tell us about...'
- the words of a Bible verse on individual cards to put in order

Give clear directions

Don't assume that the children know instinctively what's expected of them. Confusion encourages restlessness. Give instructions, check that the instructions are understood, then let them get on with it.

Be relational

We teach children, not lessons. Children are more likely to 'stay with you' when you know them and they know you.

- Pray for your class and depend on God to show himself through you. Look for God's Spirit in them as well.
- Acknowledge birthdays.
- Ask the office or class teacher which children have done something memorable and add your commendation. For example, 'Congratulations Spiro, Jeong and Claire for representing the school at the zone cross country and Theo for being elected as the school recycling officer.'
- Comment on movies they may have seen and things you see them with.
- Ask for opinions from the class and value those opinions even if they differ from yours.
- Briefly share from your own experience when appropriate.
- Watch them play sport and cheer them on.

colour

COLOUR COLOUR COLOUR COLOUR COLOUR COLOUR COLOU

Children are attracted to strong, bright colours so think of ways to colour their world!

Suggested uses

- Use coloured markers on a whiteboard and coloured chalk on a chalkboard.
- Colour your illustrations and charts.
- Print handouts on coloured paper.
- Encourage children to decorate coloured bookmarks for Bibles and other books.
- Hand out coloured paper to write on. (Commercial printers may be able to give you off-cuts from print runs.)
- Give awards of bright ribbons for behaviour that you want to encourage.
- Allow bright felt pens in group work. (Keep a spare set in your bag for children who do not have any.)
- Use 'hollow' fonts on handouts so that children can colour them in. (Some suitable fonts are *Geometric, Alphabet Soup Tilt, Stone Age* and *Castellar.* Alternatively, use the Outline effect under Format /Fonts in Word.)

Terminology

Primary colours are red, blue and yellow.

Secondary colours are made by mixing two primary colours. Secondary colours are green, orange and purple.

Complementary colours, that is green and red, blue and orange, purple and yellow are opposite on the wheel.

Warm colours contain red. Red, orange, orange-yellow are all warm colours.

Cool colours contain blue. Blue, green, greeny-yellow, purple are all cool colours.

Tone indicates the lightness or darkness of the colour.

A *tint* is the colour plus white.

A *shade* is the colour plus black.

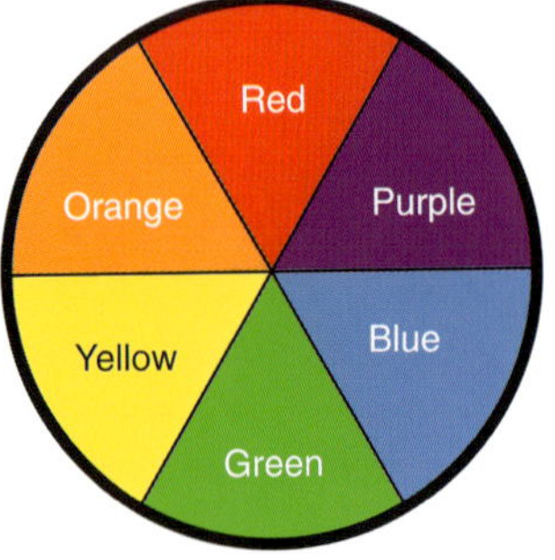

Colour wheel

Top tips for using colour

- For young children use the primary colours plus green.

- For an eye-catching combination of colour, use any pair of complementary colours. Equal amounts of these can be disturbing so use more of one than the other. For example, on a poster use a strong orange for the important words and blue for the rest of the information. Or print the text in blue and highlight with orange arrows or stars.

- Warm colours attract the eye but cool colours retreat into the background.

- Yellow is hard to read from a distance, particularly at night. Use sparingly on posters.

- To economise on printing costs, use tints and tones of one colour. This can be done on the computer. The effect is interesting if you then print on coloured paper. For example, text printed in tints and tones of blue on yellow paper will appear to be printed in various blues and greens as the paper colour will show through the lighter blues. This produces multicoloured printing at the cost of one colour printing.

- For a harmonious effect, use three adjoining colours on the colour wheel.

conclusions

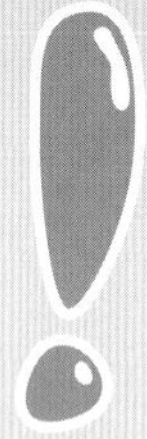

When and how you will stop needs to be well planned.
It should be more than a recapping of what's gone before.

Launching into a lengthy explanation or interpretation is a sure way to kill interest. Tacking a 'moral' on the end of a story is the signal that tells children to 'switch off' immediately. Instead, teaching and things to think about need to be woven into the structure of the story itself, so the listeners have time to think about them.

So, if you were telling the story of the healing of blind Bartimaeus in Mark 10, you could describe him throwing off his coat when called to meet Jesus. This action in verse 50 revealed the confidence he had that Jesus could heal him because blind people cannot discard their belongings in the street and really expect to find them again. For your conclusion, after describing Bartimaeus' jubilation at the restoration of his sight, you could pose the question: 'I wonder whether Bartimaeus went back to pick up his coat? Maybe he was so eager to follow Jesus that he forgot about it. Maybe a passer-by saw the coat lying there and said, 'Say, isn't that Bartimaeus' old coat? He must have forgotten it. Wasn't it amazing that Jesus was able to heal him? Jesus really must be the Son of God.'

A good conclusion satisfies the expectations aroused at the beginning. Plan your conclusion. Know what your final words are going to be, say them, then stop.

control and discipline

See also ***Classroom Management, Relationships, Venues***

We don't get far with our teaching unless we have the children's co-operation.

When the subject of 'Control and Discipline' or 'Managing Behaviour' is an elective at a children's ministry training seminar it will often draw the largest number of participants. While training sessions of this type are beneficial, there is often some degree of disappointment because the solutions discussed cannot be the answer for every situation.

Broadly speaking there are three different types of situations which call for different management strategies.

1. Informal settings which the children attend voluntarily such as after-school missions, kids' clubs and holiday clubs. These are covered in this section.

2. Formal structured settings like religious instruction in school. See *Classroom Management.*

3. Large formal structured settings like school assemblies. See *Venues.*

Team participation

Whether the function you are holding is a special event or a regular weekly after-school club, you will need trained workers who recognise they are not merely there as onlookers but have a responsibility as part of the team. This will involve them in being part of everything that happens rather than just doing their own thing until it's time for their activity.

Seating

When the children cover a wide age range, it is wise to organise for the younger children to occupy the front seats. This enables them to see better and you to control them more easily because they are the ones with the shorter attention spans.

Generally speaking, control is easier when children are seated on chairs because they are then far less mobile! Always insist that children have their own chair. You are making trouble for yourself if you permit two to cram onto the same chair, or if you allow an older child to hold a younger one. If you are the compere, train other team members to notice and curb undesirable behaviour so you don't make yourself unpopular by ordering people about before the programme begins.

As children arrive, play light, soothing music to settle them down. Some children will rush to fill the front seats; others, usually the older ones, may file into the back rows. If, as a result, there are empty rows in the centre, ask those at the rear to move forward. The team should immediately move in to remove the empty seats, leaving just enough to cater for any latecomers. This gives a tidier feel to the assembled group. Your team should be ready to direct latecomers to a place unobtrusively.

Begin with a fanfare

Don't be perturbed by the normal excited chatter of the children as they are coming in and getting settled. Time your moment when you call them to order and introduce your first activity without fuss. This can be an opening song, but a visual quiz game may be more generally popular.

While you want an enthusiastic start, avoid pointless whipping up of enthusiasm.

'Hullo, boys and girls!'
'Hullo.'
'What? I can't hear you!'
'HULLO!'

Anyone with experience in handling bees will know that it is unwise to stir them up and the same holds true for large groups of children. Once the children reach screaming pitch, time is wasted in the struggle to settle them down again.

Control from the front

Nothing undermines a gathering more than some adult chiming in from the sidelines and scolding the children for inattention. Ideally, a team member should promptly and unobtrusively deal with nearby inattention trouble spots. When this doesn't happen, the person who is leading must be aware of trouble spots and deal with them. This may be done by gaining the attention of the child who is being disruptive. It is important not to ignore escalating inattention because it can spread rapidly.

There may be some deliberately disruptive children. If eye contact fails to deter them, it may be necessary to take firmer action for the benefit of the whole group. Move the offender to a seat at the end of a rear row where they will be less disruptive. If then as a last resort, it becomes necessary to send the child out, it will cause less disturbance to the group to extract the offending child from the rear, than if they have to stumble over a row of feet in clear view of all the other children.

At one after-school club, the children were fidgeting and giggling and the leader was becoming more and more irritated. In his exasperation, he began to pray very loudly that Satan would be rebuked. Having prayed in this way he then berated the children for their misbehaviour in 'the house of God.' Perhaps the leader was more to blame than the children. He had commenced the meeting with a boisterous song that stirred them up. While they were singing, instead of giving the lead, he walked off to the side to chat with one of his team. Inevitably, the children became bored and fidgety, until the leader attempted to gain control of the children by losing his own self-control! (Satan didn't have to do much at all.)

Woo them

Those whose ministry is primarily to adults can easily lose sight of the need to capture, and maintain, the attention of children. With groups of children, it is important to be alert to every child. As you address them, the aim is to actively project your personality in such a way that each child feels that you are specifically speaking to them. Keep your eyes moving over the whole group but not so fast that you do not look each child in the eye, at least momentarily. Notice the children who are distracted by something, and concentrate your attention on them until they become aware of you, and their attention is drawn back to you. Varying the tone and volume of your voice may redirect their attention to you.

When working as a team, never leave the leader's position empty. When it is your turn to participate move into the children's sight before your predecessor has left it, saying or doing things to woo their attention as you do so.

Evaluation

If you have a troublesome session with a group of children, don't blame them (or Satan). The first thing to do is to check up on yourself. You are the one who influences what happens most. Ask yourself:

Was I too busy to prepare properly?
Was I too tired or lacking in enthusiasm?
Was the programme boring?
What should be done to make the programme more appealing?
Did the meeting drag?
Did the introduction kindle interest?
When did the group begin to lose interest?
Was each team member adequately briefed beforehand?

Whatever your answers to the previous questions, if you have a troublesome session, make as many changes as you can for the next. Move some of the furniture. If the seating was in straight rows, curve the rows or set them at an angle. Change the positions of the board, the screen, the puppet theatre and anything else that moves. The purpose is to indicate that last session is over and this one will be different. Tighten up control from the outset, perhaps by insisting that the children file in, in a more orderly fashion. Start promptly and keep the function rolling along with 'unhurried haste'.

When the 'outlook' is grim, try the 'up-look'. Pray! It is often when we reach the end of our abilities that we prove God's enabling.

copyright

Look for materials that are produced for you to copy.

As a general rule, it is illegal to reproduce by hand by photocopying or by printing any published material – including songs and drama scripts – without prior permission of the publisher. Check the small print details next to the copyright notice for what is legal for the publication you're interested in. Don't assume that because something is copyright a publisher will refuse permission to copy, but you must ask.

Music can also be performed or played by a teacher or student to give or receive instruction, provided it is not for profit and it is only viewed by those participating in the instruction (not a performance to an audience).

For further information regarding copyright requirements in churches, helpful websites are www.copyright.org.au. and www.copyright.org.uk

craft

A well planned craft activity can achieve the following objectives

Reinforced teaching	Making boats out of polystyrene, paper and satay skewers could be used to reinforce the storm incident in Mark 4.
Variety in the programme	Craft provides a contrast with other activities and children love making things.
Icebreaking	Rather than children standing round waiting for a programme to start, they can begin a craft project and complete it later.
Providing an opportunity ...	for skills and talents of children and leaders to be expressed.
Informal discussion time ...	between leaders and children while they make something together.
A chance for leaders to show care ...	as they lend a hand.

The list of practical projects is endless. Talk with people who enjoy craft. Research books, craft magazines, curriculum materials and specialist suppliers. Check out crafts for children on the Internet.

Top tips for craft

- **Gather people** who enjoy doing craft to provide help and ideas. Often people who won't be involved in teaching or games are keen to get their hands all gluey!

- **Be prepared** for spills and accidents. A good supply of wet wipes, garbage bags, paper towels and drop sheets relieve the stress. Allow time for cleanup of children and the working space. A set of aprons or paint shirts may be useful.

- **Attach the child's name** to everything they make. Named paper plates are good drying trays and useful for carrying crafts home.

- **Plan for those who will finish quickly.** What will they do when they finish early and others are still going? One idea is to have an on-going project, such as a series of banners or a painted backdrop for the church or hall.

- **Allow time for paint and glue to dry.**
  Provide safe storage if the project requires more than one session.

- **Provide robust and useful projects** for older children, especially boys. Projects made from leather (key rings and backpack tags) or wood (bookends or pre-cut boxes) are interesting.

- **Always allow for successful completion.** Children lose heart if they have worked hard on something and they can't complete it. You may have to fast track slow workers. Think carefully about on-going projects if children may not return another day.

design

See also ***Advertising, Colour, Publicity***

Design improves the appearance of the materials you produce and helps you deliver information effectively.

For publicity brochures, posters, charts and handouts, design is closely related to layout which is the arrangement of your material.

Before you apply design, you will need to gather your information (see *Publicity*).
Your items of information, listed in order of importance, are the elements of your design.

Planning your design

Sketch roughly several ideas for the layout in small, quickly done drawings.

These sketches are called 'thumbnail' sketches. Choose the one you like best. Even if you are working on a computer, these little thumbnails help you formulate your ideas so the layout does not happen haphazardly. Use scribbles to indicate lines of writing.

To achieve an interesting result, use the following basic principles of design to arrange the elements.

Shape	Think of your blocks of text in terms of shapes – rectangles and squares. Arrange them on the page. These blocks form the elements of your design. (See thumbnails 6-10.)
Balance	Don't let your elements form a lop-sided design on the page. Look carefully and make sure the areas of writing are not crowded at the top or bottom of the page. A group of light-weight lines will balance off one heavy line. (See thumbnails 3 and 5.)
Focal point	This focuses the eye to the main message which is usually the title of the function. Make this the heaviest, darkest lettering and keep plenty of white space around it. It is often best placed at about one-third from the top of the page.
Contrast	Use a change of font, colour, texture, tone or shape of text areas.
Repetition	Repeat the use of font, shape or colour.
Movement	Add 'movement' in the design by putting a line at an angle. (See thumbnail 4.)
Space	Leave space around the page and between the elements. Space gives a place for the eye to rest and cuts down confusion.

Start off simply and get more adventurous with your designs. Remember always that cluttered designs are ineffective. One form of clutter is to have more than three font types. Varying the size and boldness of those few you choose will give all the variety you need. Keep it clear and simple!

dialogue

Dialogue is very important in enabling your audience to imagine the characters when storytelling.

When you describe a character in terms of height, weight and even eye colour, people will still have little understanding of the type of person he is. Personality is demonstrated by what people do, what they say, and what is said about them not just what they look like.

Sometimes storytellers need only to repeat the dialogue that occurs in the biblical text but, in most cases, you must use your imagination to expand it.

Use direct speech – Isaac's wife

A simple method for developing dialogue is to take the details that are reported in narrative form in the Bible passage and switch them into speech. For example, much of the account of the search by Abraham's servant for a wife for Isaac is in narrative. Genesis 24:28 says simply that the girl ran and told her mother's household about these things. It could be expressed in dialogue as

'Mother, mother! Look what I've got!'

'What is it, Rebekah?'

'A golden nose ring and two golden bracelets!'

'What? Where did you get them?'

'From a man – a man I met at the well. He – he asked me for a drink and I gave him some of my water and drew water for his camels as well.'

'Was he by himself?'

'No! He had servants with him, and a whole string of camels. He asked whether there would be room here at our house for them to stay.'

'Oh, did he now?'

'He asked which family I belonged to. When I told him Dad's name was Bethuel and that Grandad's name was Nahor, he fell down on the ground and worshipped the Lord. He mentioned the God of Abraham!'

'Abraham? Goodness me, that's Nahor's brother. Quickly, Laban! Run and see who this fellow is, and why he has given your sister these valuable presents. If he has come from Abraham, you must invite him to our home at once!'

None of this conversation is recorded in Scripture and yet it must be very close to what was said at the time. When you change narrative into dialogue, you heighten interest in the story.

Use repetition – the Samaritan lepers

In Elisha's time four leprous men returned to the besieged city of Samaria with the news that the surrounding army had fled. The narrative is recorded in 2 Kings 7 but the dialogue may have been like this. We've made it more colloquial, remembering that any English Bible version is a translation.

> 'Your majesty, your majesty! The gatekeepers have reported that some lepers have come to tell us the enemy has fled.'
>
> 'It's a trap! The enemy knows how weak we are. They know we are starving. They have left their camp to hide in the hills. They think we'll rush down to their camp to get food and they'll capture us alive and get into the city'.
>
> 'B-but your majesty, what if it's true? What if they really have gone?'
>
> 'No! No way! I'm awake to their little scheme. They'll be hiding in ambush hoping we'll rush down to their camp and leave the city unguarded. They'll be able to capture us if we do that, and they'll get into the city.'
>
> 'Sir, just in case it's true, won't you order some of the men to take a couple of our chariots and check it out?'

Note that the king's speech from 2 Kings 7:12 has been expanded by being repeated.

Use expansion

Dialogue in the scriptures will, in many cases, be a condensation, so an expansion of the biblical text has a good chance of being nearer the reality of the event. Compare this conversation with the report in 2 Kings 7:3-4.

> 'I can't stand this any longer!'
>
> 'What are you talking about?'
>
> 'The pain of an empty stomach. It's killing me.'
>
> 'So what do you want us to do about it?'
>
> 'I don't know. But there must be something we can do instead of just sitting here getting weaker and weaker.'

'Perhaps we could go back to the city. I've got friends in there who might throw us some food over the wall.'

'Bah! What's the sense in that. They're starving, too. Last I heard they were eating donkey heads, *if* they could buy one.' *(Silence for a few seconds.)*

'I know where there's plenty of food!'

'Where?'

'In the enemy camp!'

'Ha! Smart, aren't you. How could we get that?'

'We could just go over there and surrender. They might spare our lives, but if they kill us, we'll only die! And we're going do that anyway.'

'Hmmm. If they kill us it will be quicker and less painful than dying of hunger. I'm willing to give it a go. What about you?'

'Of course, I suggested it, didn't I? And what about you other guys?'

'Might as well! It's a good deal when you've got nothing to lose! Come on, let's all go! Will someone give me a hand up?'

Use volume and pitch changes

When reporting dialogue there are times when the storyteller will lift the voice to give it greater volume. For example, *Athaliah tore her robes and shouted, 'TREASON! TREASON!'* (2 Chronicles 23:13) At other times the dialogue may be a loud whisper. For instance, we can be certain that the woman in Luke 8:47 who touched Jesus' robe would not have been shouting when she confessed to what she had done. In reporting her speech we may even break it up with stammers and sobs, noting that the woman was terrified.

'I-I was the one *(Sob)* who did it. I saw you passing and-and I knew that if *(Sob)* I could touch you, I-I would be healed. And-and I was right! The illness that has plagued me for twelve years is gone.'

At times a male storyteller should lift the normal frequency of his voice to a higher pitch for a woman's or a child's part. Similarly a female storyteller should drop the frequency of her voice if speaking an adult male's part. The effectiveness of your dialogue will also be enhanced if you change the quality of your voice to indicate such aspects as arrogance, compassion, uncertainty, sorrow and old age.

See also ***Script writing***

Drama plays a significant part in each of our lives. Not only do we have dramatic moments in our everyday experience, but we also spend considerable time either reading about, or watching, the dramatic experiences of others.

In children's ministry, there are two main categories:

A production where children are the actors

Most children enjoy dressing up and performing, although usually girls are less self-conscious than boys and find it easier to participate.

Drama can be handled in different ways.

- The children mime the actions while an adult or a competent reader narrates. A Christmas pageant for little children can be an example of this. While from a dramatic point of view it is rather tame, the children get a lot of pleasure from it.
- The children are trained to perform a play, speaking to a simplified script. This can be successful as long as sufficient opportunity for practice is available beforehand. Some children remember for years the dialogue they learned for a school play.
- As a compromise, acting notes or speech parts can be written on cards held by the children, perhaps hidden in hands or on properties.

A production by adults where children are the audience

- This can be a brief skit usually involving two people.
- A teacher takes the part of a character recounting his or her experience in the first person. Dressing up enhances this performance.
- Actors learn their parts from a prepared script and perform with both action and recited dialogue.
- The entire story is narrated while others mime. Sandy Galea in her book *Children's Talks: A Practical Guide* calls this 'mugs drama'. The actors simply act out what the narrator says. If dialogue is needed, the narrator can say: 'And the king called "Send for Daniel."' Then actor playing the king repeats 'Send for Daniel.'

Ideas for dramas

- Bible stories
- Christian classics like *Pilgrim's Progress, The Lion the Witch and the Wardrobe, Treasures of the Snow* and *Papa Panov.*
- Incidents from history such as the story of King Christian X of Denmark who substituted for his sentry. The German commandant in charge of the occupation of Copenhagen had threatened that the sentry at the palace would be shot at sundown unless the Danish flag was taken down. When the Germans discovered the sentry on duty was King Christian, they didn't dare shoot him, and the Danish flag continued to fly.
- True stories that illustrate a biblical parable. It could be a story of a treasure hunter who risked everything to find a lost treasure ship.
- Parables in a different context. An example would be the Good Samaritan in a contemporary setting as a bikie.
- Original stories. While this is undoubtedly the most difficult, it's good to remind ourselves that every classic was once new and original.

dvd / video clips

Movie clips can be used to illustrate a point, add variety or introduce new themes and concepts. Here is a list of themes and movies to start you off.

Counting the cost	*Men in Black* Will Smith asks Tommy Lee Jones about giving up his old life to become an agent.
Grace	*Les Miserables* The bishop produces the candlesticks.
Leadership	*Chicken Run* Ginger gives hope when she imparts vision to the other chickens.
Protection	*Harry Potter and the Philosopher's Stone* Dumbledore explains that Harry could not be touched by evil because love has left its mark on him.
Sacrifice	*Beauty and the Beast* Belle gives up her freedom and her father and remains with the beast.
Self image	*Shrek 2* Princess Fiona dislikes handsome Prince Charming posing as the new Shrek. Shrek and Fiona choose to retain their ogre form.
Sovereignty	*Joseph King of Dreams* The gaol scene and song 'You know better than I' illustrate God's direction of history.
Seeking the lost	*Finding Nemo* Nemo's father goes to extraordinary lengths to find his son.
Temptation	*The Lion King* Simba is tempted by Scar to go to the elephants' graveyard.

Graham Wade has also created a series of videos entitled *Scribbly Yarns* which explore biblical concepts. These videos are available for purchase and can be sourced through Internet search engines.

Life's aim	*Boomerang* video 5
Sacrifice	*Swaggie* video 1
Service	*The Macarthur's* video 4

Check out recent movies at the website www.hollywoodjesus.com for reviews and spiritual links.

Open-air presentations require a very stable board which cannot be blown off the easel.

This one is the most effective. It does have limitations, however, namely, that you need a van or a roof rack to transport it. Should you need something more easily transportable, an art supply shop can supply you with one with telescopic legs and a folding board or, if this is beyond the range of your pocket, a home carpenter may be able to construct what you need.

The outer legs

1. Cut three lengths from 18 mm by 70 mm timber. The two outer legs should be 1700 mm long. The inner leg should be longer; the length is determined by the slope of the board and what is most comfortable for you.

2. Obtain a piece of 13 mm steel rod about 190 mm long by 50 mm diameter. Flatten the ends and drill a bolt hole through each flattened end.

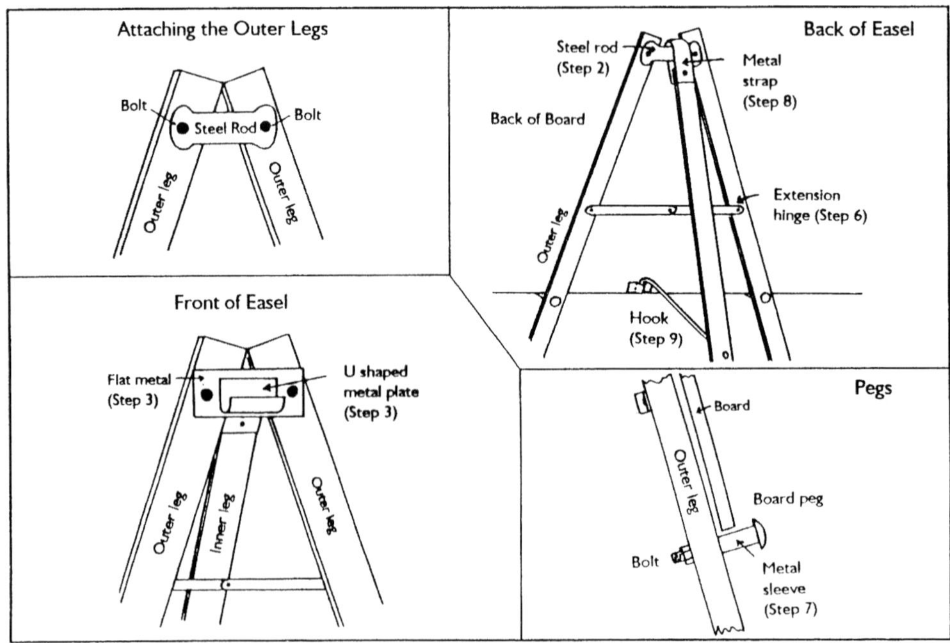

3. Take another piece of metal, this time a flat piece 190 mm long and 50 mm wide. Drill a hole in each end in the same position as the holes in the steel rod. At the midpoint in this metal piece, weld a U-shaped metal plate (about 70 mm long by 40 mm wide) to form a hook. (Later this hook will be connected to a flange piece on the back of the board.)

4. Drill a hole through the middle of the top of each outer leg about 55 mm from the end.

5. Screw a bolt through the end hole of each leg – first through the flat metal piece with the hook, next through the wood and then the metal rod.

6. Attach an extension hinge (a smaller version of those used on aluminium ladders) about 600 mm from the top end of the legs to keep the legs apart when open.

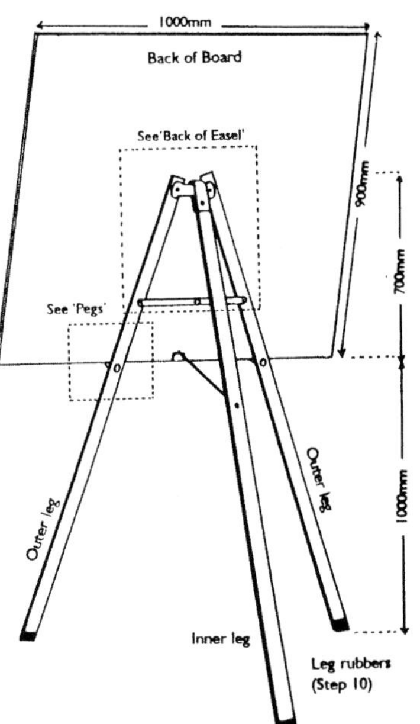

The board

7. Fit a large bolt to each leg, 1000 mm from the bottom (floor level). Using a metal sleeve, make the bolt head protrude by 20 mm. This creates a 'peg' on which the board will sit. The board should be 1100 mm by 900 mm and thick enough to always remain rigid.

8. Obtain a piece of flat metal similar to the piece used in step 3 and make a bend in it to take the hook. Attach this piece to the back of the board in the correct position for the hook.

The inner leg

9. Fit a metal strap to the top of the inner leg forming a loop over the rod holding the outer legs.

10. A long hook from the rear leg to the back of the board will prevent the rear leg from slipping.

11. Fit chair rubbers to the feet of your easel legs to give further stability if used on a slippery floor.

embellishment

When we unnecessarily or inappropriately embellish the details of Bible stories, we replace scriptural truths by fiction and this can work against children gaining saving faith.

Christian faith is not believing in the unknown or unrevealed; it is trusting in the revealed person of Christ.

The events surrounding the birth of Jesus have suffered most in this respect. At an infants school assembly, the speaker focused her entire address on the donkey that Mary rode to Bethlehem. There is no reference whatever to a donkey in the gospels; very probably Mary walked all the way. In some instances, embellishments can be traced to the artists who have portrayed the events. The Magi (wise men) are invariably depicted as a trio riding camels whereas, however many they were, they may have walked too!

This problem is not confined to the Christmas story. Many a story lesson on 'the boy who gave his lunch to Jesus' has portrayed him as the most important person in the incident and his action presented as an example for others to follow. The gospels, however, give him no such prominence. Only one of the four gospel accounts mentions him at all.

While it is important not to overlook details that make the story live, beware of going to the other extreme of making too much of something minor. There are two allowable reasons for a storyteller to expand the biblical text:

Include the probable causes of known effects

A good example to explain this would be the account of David's warriors attacking the Philistines to get their king a drink of water (2 Samuel 23:16). What we are told is that they broke through the Philistine lines. What preceded this? The storyteller can describe them buckling on their armour and preparing themselves for the battle ahead. This is probable. They would not have attempted the task without such preparations.

Include the probable effects of known causes

When Rebekah agreed to go with Abraham's servant to become Isaac's wife what thoughts would have tumbled through her mind? Perhaps she said to her family 'I wonder what this Isaac will be like as a husband'.

Accuracy above all

Children's workers have frequently been heard to say, 'Jesus said such and such…' when there is no record of such a statement in the gospels. They are more likely to be expressing ideas that are found in the epistles. Some will argue that, because the epistles are the Word of God, we can attribute them to the Lord Jesus. Many theologians, however, regard Paul's expressions of the gospel as quite different from those of Jesus, so it is preferable to say 'Paul said' or 'Peter said' rather than attribute a statement falsely to the Lord himself. If we preached a sermon to adults and made an incorrect statement, someone would probably point out our error. Because the audience we are addressing is children, who are unlikely to notice, it does not give us licence to put words into the Lord's mouth; rather we have a responsibility to be even more careful with the truth.

enthusiasm

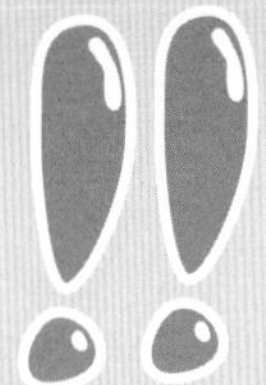

See also ***Participation, Zest***

Children inevitably respond to enthusiasm. Lack of enthusiasm is often the reason that an activity which fails miserably for one leader, is a real hit for another. Beware of being too 'laid back' or 'low key' in your approach.

> Camp Conqueror is a bushwalking camp based at Milton on the south coast of NSW, Australia. The leaders of this camp had what could be called a 'second preference mentality'. For several years the camp failed to attract sufficient numbers of first choice applicants, and so it had come to depend on the overflow of applicants from other camps to fill its numbers. A new leader set out to correct this negative attitude. He began by inventing a slogan which was painted in large letters in a prominent place at the campsite: 'Conqueror, the Camp with Class'.
>
> Next, the programme from previous years was examined and a new schedule of activities planned. The team members were somewhat taken aback when repeatedly reminded by the leader, 'We can't do that! You did that last year!'
>
> When the camp started that next summer, the team was determined to let the campers know that it was under new management. They were told how fortunate they were to have chosen to come to 'the best camp ever'. Perhaps this title was a rather ambitious claim, but what it did was express an attitude.
>
> The camp had its problems, and some of the campers resisted the changes initially but, by the time the camp ended, the doubters had been won over. The following summer, Camp Conqueror was the first camp to fill its quota and had to send some of the late applicants off to other camps.

When a programme or a camp is being run by a team, it is essential that all its members are equally enthusiastic. The leader must be approachable and seek to encourage the team at every opportunity. Taking their suggestions seriously will help to keep them enthusiastic.

Of course, it is not only the leaders that need to be enthusiastic, but the children as well. Including them in planning and helping will give them a sense of belonging and teamwork. In regular weekly activities, such as after-school clubs, it's good to appoint jobs to some of the children to encourage them to participate enthusiastically. Within safety and care guidelines, children can help keep the registrations, move tables, set out seats, operate the overhead projector and do many other tasks.

eye contact

Clear eye communication between the speaker and everyone in the audience is essential. If something hinders that communication, change whatever is necessary. Especially with children, if you don't give the impression that you are talking to them, they cannot be blamed if they 'switch off'.

> A new teacher was having constant difficulty in controlling her class. Her programme was up-to-date and well planned. Her visuals were exceptionally well produced. She appeared to be outgoing and confident. Despite this, every lesson was a riot. The deputy principal was given the task of discovering the reason for her problem. The answer was not difficult to find. When the teacher addressed the class, she stared at a point somewhere in the distance above their heads. Aware of this, the members of her class could wriggle and chatter as they pleased. Once the problem was identified as lack of eye contact, action was possible to help her to correct it.

When speaking, keep your head up, look towards the centre of the group and speak out clearly. Give your audience the feeling that you are speaking personally to each one of them.

While eye contact is an important factor in class control, it's important for another reason. Alert speakers will watch carefully, assessing the children's interest level and adjusting their delivery if necessary.

What do you do when you need to take a session based on a Bible story that the group is already over-familiar with?

If you look carefully enough, you'll find unusual angles in the familiar Bible narratives. But beware of such solutions as telling the Palm Sunday story from the point of view of the donkey! Such angles rob you of the opportunity of treating Jesus and his claims seriously. Study the Bible passage carefully once more and see if you can answer the questions it raises for you. Consider how it links with the life situation of your audience.

Palm Sunday

Here's a suggested outline based on the coming of Jesus to Jerusalem on Palm Sunday and the reactions of the people who saw him. It was constructed after reading the account in all four gospels looking for a new angle.

Four groups of people are mentioned.

1. People who didn't understand

They asked 'Who is this?' (Matt 21:10).

2. People who knew who Jesus was

They had seen Lazarus being raised from death and this convinced them that Jesus was the Son of God (John 12:17).

3. People who were annoyed

The Pharisees asked Jesus to silence the enthusiastic crowd (Luke 19:39).

4. People who were interested

The Greek onlookers requested an introduction to Jesus (John 12:20).

Older children who are familiar with the story could well be fascinated if you tackle it beginning with the prophecy of Jesus concerning the overthrow of Jerusalem (Luke 19:41-44) and the subsequent fulfilment in AD 70 when the Roman army under Titus marched into the city.

Another angle you could explore would be to trace the effects that the events had upon Jesus' enemies. All the gospel writers mention those effects.

first person recital

This storytelling technique involves taking the part of a character in the story. Dress up and tell the story as the character would tell it, in the first person. Another team member can introduce you as the character and perhaps conduct an interview later, asking questions like 'You met Jesus. What's he really like?'

First person presenters can be either major or minor characters, or even imaginary bystanders. It is important for the character to be maintained throughout. The person must not lapse into the present by preaching an explanation of their behaviour.

Another way a first person recital can be presented is with an overhead projector. The facial image of the person recounting the experience is projected with a series of pictures that are added to the speech balloon as the recital proceeds. Below is a picture to represent the Philippian jailer. After you enlarge them, the overlay pictures can either be hinged to the sides of the frame or else left free to be lifted on and off as the story progresses.

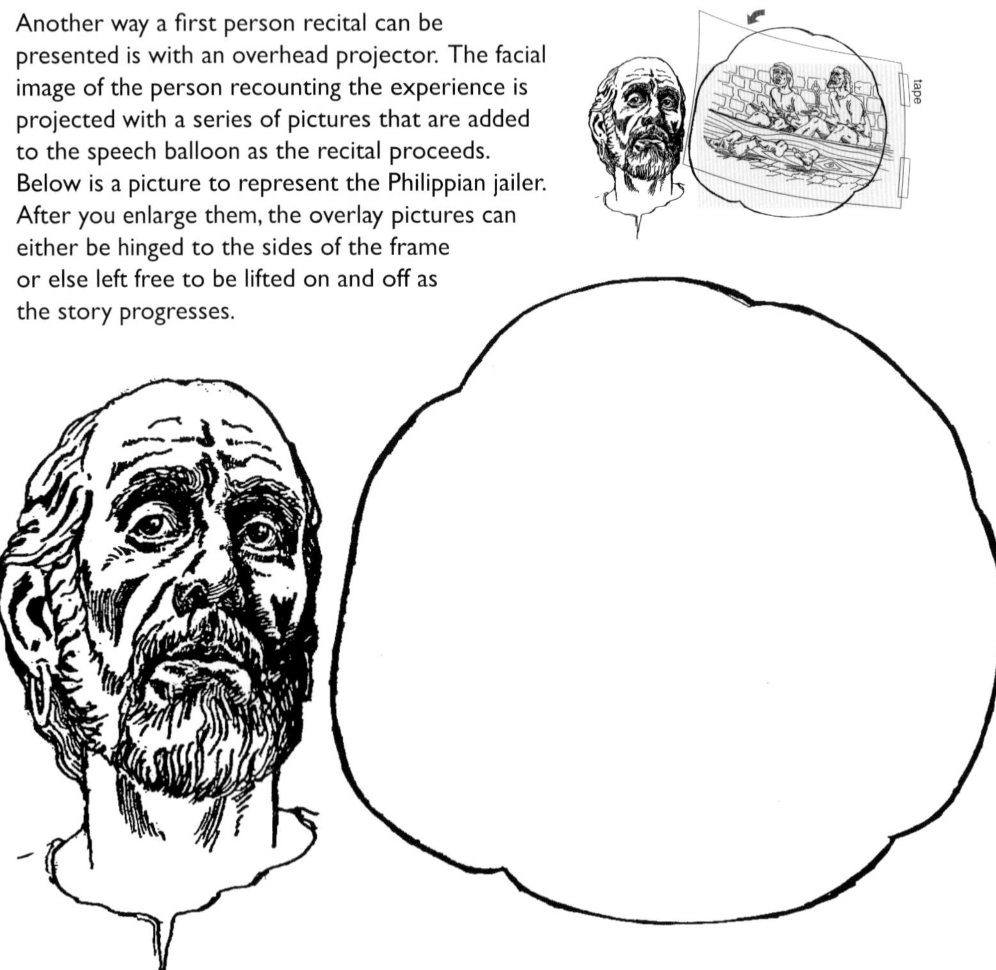

2

Hinge here

Believe in the Lord Jesus and you will be saved

5

Hinge here

3

Hinge here

Hinge here

4

1

flashcard pictures

This method of presentation involves showing a series of pictures as the story is recounted. These can be drawn on sheets of paper which are attached to a board and exposed one by one as the story progresses.

Alternatively they can be made into transparencies for use on an overhead projector, or on cards that can be 'flashed' in turn. Experience teaches that five or six pictures are needed for maintaining interest. Fewer than that, and each picture needs to be held up for too long, losing its impact.

Picture talk – the crucifixion

Here is an outline which views the crucifixion from a different angle, to stimulate the interest of older children who may think they know the story well.

Aim

To demonstrate that Jesus was innocent of any wrongdoing.

Introduction

You are standing outside the school waiting for the bus when 'screech, crash'; right in front of your eyes you see a huge truck smash into a little car. Soon, a police car arrives. When the police find out that you saw it all happen, they ask for your name and address. You have become an 'eyewitness'. Later you will be asked to attend the trial and tell what you saw.

There may also be other witnesses who were not at the scene of a crime. They can be called on to give testimony about the person who has been arrested. These are called 'character witnesses'. Here are five people, character witnesses, who had something to say about Jesus at the time of his arrest.

Enlarge and colour the five pictures of hands on the following pages to illustrate your talk.

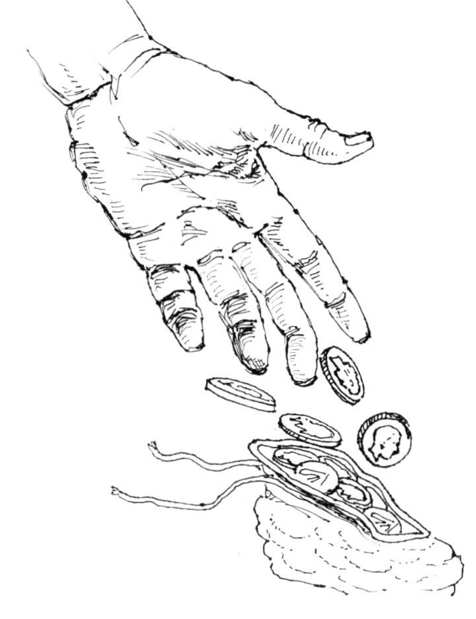

1. Judas

This one used to be a friend of Jesus. This is the hand of the disciple who betrayed Jesus. What was his name? Judas was bribed by the Jewish leaders to betray the Lord Jesus. How much money was he paid? Recount Judas returning the money in Matthew 27:3-5. When Judas spoke about Jesus, he described him as 'innocent'. What does innocent mean? Discuss.

2. Pilate's wife

The second witness is a very strange one. Pontius Pilate was the Roman governor at the time of the trial of the Lord Jesus. As he was listening to the accusations that were made, the trial was interrupted by a messenger. Pilate had been asked to hold the trial of Jesus very early in the morning. After he left home, his wife tried to go back to sleep but her thoughts troubled her (Matthew 27: 19). She sent a message to her husband which read

Don't have anything to do with that innocent man. I have had nightmares because of him.

Pilate's wife must have heard about the Lord Jesus to describe him as 'innocent'.

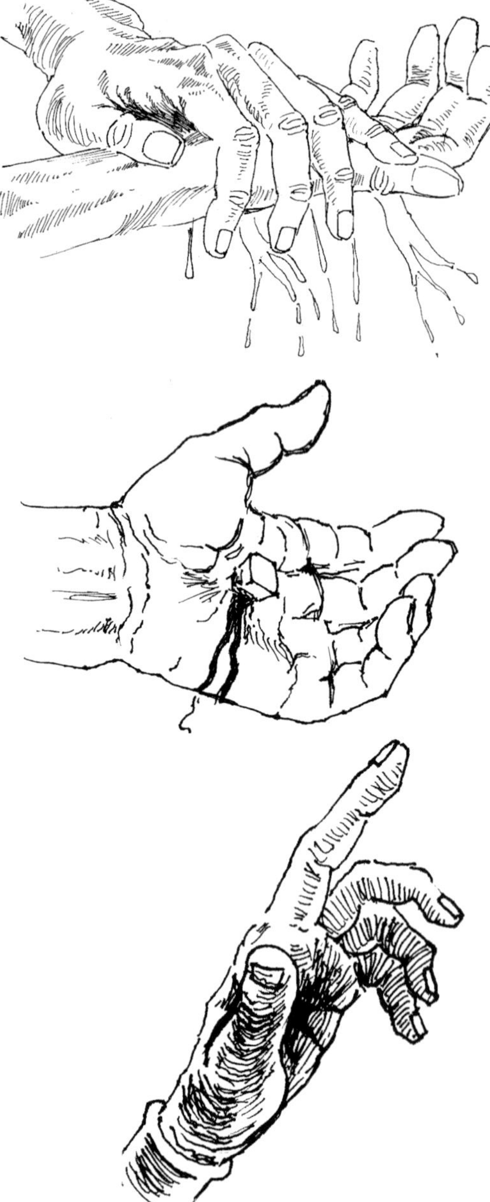

3. Pontius Pilate

Pontius Pilate wasn't silly. As he listened to the accusations that were made against Jesus, he realised that they were all false. Calling for a basin of water, he washed his hands (Matthew 27:23-24). His verdict was

I don't find this man guilty of anything (John 18:38).

4. The thief

Reporting the conversation between the thieves, the primary focus is on the thief's testimony to the character of Jesus:

This man has done nothing wrong (Luke 23:41).

5 The army captain

The centurion was a soldier in charge of a hundred men. He'd probably seen lots of men killed. His testimony is:

Surely this was a righteous man (Luke 23:47).

Conclusion

All these people knew that Jesus was innocent. What about us? Which of us would be described by our enemies as innocent and good like Jesus? Even our friends wouldn't say that about us. We have all been guilty of things like telling lies, cheating, being selfish, cruel or proud. The good news is that, through the death of Jesus, who was innocent, we will be forgiven when we ask him.

flexibility

Outdoor events and weather

One summer at Shoal Bay, NSW, as starting time for one of the beach meetings approached, weather conditions didn't look promising. Dark clouds were rolling in from the southwest and thunder rumbled menacingly in the distance. Noticing that most of the audience had already gathered, the team decided to make an early start. Fearing that people would desert the programme when the storm hit, it was arranged for the speaker to commence straight after the opening song. The team hoped that the storm would be delayed long enough for him to give his message. As the sky grew darker and the thunder drew closer, he pressed on, valiantly ignoring the threatened downpour. Slowly the clouds rolled over and the rumbles subsided without a single drop of rain falling. By the time the speaker had finished, the sun was shining, and the storm had passed. All the other scheduled parts of the meeting followed. The order of events was a complete reversal of what was planned, but everything was still included.

On another occasion, this time at Evans Head on the east coast of Australia, a tropical storm sent the team, and the families who had gathered, running to a large shelter. After the early intensity of the storm had eased, someone led some singing and the speaker for the day gave his message standing on one of the picnic tables. Much of the programme had to be abandoned, but the important bit was still shared and a good time was had by all.

Uneven starts

The team leader at one children's church group had difficulty arriving on time each week because he was transporting community children. To overcome this difficulty, he arranged for another leader to read part of CS Lewis' story *The Lion, the Witch and the Wardrobe* until he arrived. The children were free to either listen to the reading or to play outside. While most of the children opted for the story, a few of the boys preferred to play. This arrangement was warmly received by the children who all co-operated well.

Adjusting the programme

If you sense that some part of the programme is failing to grip the attention of your audience, be prepared to cut it short. On the other hand, it's good to have some activities ready to include if the programme is moving faster than expected.

At a school Easter assembly, as the children filed into the assembly hall, a brawl broke out that was only quelled with some vigorous shouting by the staff. The resultant atmosphere was unsettling and the speaker, sensing that his planned talk had become quite unsuitable, switched to another. He still used his sketch board, but the illustrations were very simple and did not require him to turn from the group to sketch for more than a few seconds at a time. In this situation, the children needed his undivided attention.

Games are an important ingredient of most children's programmes and we ought not to view them merely as time-fillers or as opportunities for the children to let off steam. Through games, we have an opportunity to teach and model Christian values.

The attitude of the leader

When you are the person responsible for directing the games, the participants want you to be someone who is both decisive and fair. Many a session has been spoilt by squabbles over rules. State the rules clearly, then get on with it. It's very frustrating to children, when the leader is undecided. Sensitivity is another attitude of a good leader. Not all children are enthusiastic about playing games, and you may need to allow some children to sit and watch.

The make-up of the group

The type of game you organise will depend largely on the make-up of the group. Games that are suitable for a senior boys' camp will obviously be different from those for a mixed group of younger children. Where possible, separate the infants from those of primary school age. Even among the infants, there may be some who are physically advanced and who scorn a game such as *What's the Time, Mr Wolf* which is usually popular with little people. Such children will appreciate it if you allow them to play a more boisterous game with the older children. The key is awareness of the preferences of individual children.

Choosing a game

Safety and care are prime considerations, not just in the physical sense but also to ensure that children don't feel put down or inferior because they are not good at games.

In many of our programmes, the amount of time allocated to games is limited, so choose games to keep explanations and changing teams to a minimum. In a holiday club setting, choose similar types of games for one day's session. For example on Day 1 choose games based on rules requiring the players to run around a circle. Day 2 may be a variety of relays. Day 3 could all be games that require lines of opposing teams, and so on. This saves wasting time changing from one pattern of play to another.

In elimination games, there is no need to play to the end before saying 'Right, everybody back in again!' This prevents the game time being boring to those who are 'out' early. Otherwise, plan something for those no longer in the game.

A radically different approach to games is given in an illustrated book *Everyone's a Winner!* by Ruth Willis. It contains over 200 co-operative games that are collaborative, enormous fun and designed to build up participants rather than make them feel inadequate.

An example of a co-operative game is *Skin the Snake*. The players stand in a long line holding hands. At the starting signal, the first player bends down and crawls through the legs of the second player, still holding that player's hand. What the group is seeking to achieve is for the whole group to follow through the legs without getting tangled or breaking hands. If desired, more than one team can do it at the same time, thus making a race of it. A three-legged race is an old timer that requires co-operation between the players.

Revitalising games

Familiar games that are losing their edge can be revitalised by introducing a variation to the usual rules. For instance, in the traditional *Dog and the Bone*, a player who grabs the 'bone' and is tipped by his opponent before reaching the line, is out. A variation is that they be required to drop the 'bone' and attempt to grab it again. In this case, the contest doesn't conclude until one of the players reaches the opposing team's line without being tipped.

In games where individuals are matched against each other, the leader must have the contestants as evenly matched as possible, otherwise the contest loses its appeal, especially to those who are easily beaten. Two children who appear to be similar in size may be quite different when it comes to games ability, and you may need to reallocate children to different teams to get a better balance. Be careful to make the changes a matter of 'administration' rather than individual inadequacy so that the weaker players do not feel belittled.

Collecting games

Have a variety of games that can be used in different situations. You may be called upon to direct indoor games at a youth night or you may want to run a 'wide game' at a camp. Rather than relying on your memory, operate a file in which games can be recorded.

In regular kids' clubs there is time for children to develop a liking for familiar games. In special activities, like a holiday club, use games that are unfamiliar to the children because your purpose is to give the feel that this programme is excitingly different. As with everything else in our ministry with children and young people, variety is paramount. Finally, note the participants' reactions. If you sense that the game you are directing is being received lukewarmly, don't persist with it; switch to something likely to be more appealing. While there must be hundreds of games that have been developed over the years, there is still scope for you to invent your own.

Outdoor game for a small space

The following game was invented when the available games area was restricted to a small triangular courtyard. It sounds too simple but it was very popular with the children in a situation in which many would have said there was no hope of running active games. Sufficient circles were drawn on the concrete so that each player had a circle only big enough for one to stand in. One of the children was chosen to be the catcher. When the leader called 'change', all the players had to leave their circles and run to another. A player who was tipped while running between circles was considered to be caught and had to help the catcher. The game concluded when everyone was caught. Making it a rule that players could not return to a circle which they had previously occupied, added further variety to the game.

Reviving games

Sometimes a game that was popular with earlier generations can be revived. Here is one such game with very simple rules.

Countries Each player is given the name of a country. One player throws a ball up and calls out the name of a country. The player owning that name must chase the ball while all the others scatter. On retrieving the ball, that player calls 'stop'. Immediately all must stand still. The player with the ball is permitted three steps towards the nearest player and then tosses the ball in an attempt to hit that player. If the player who had the ball is unsuccessful in hitting another, they throw the ball up and call a country's name; if successful, the hit player becomes the next caller/thrower. If a player catches the ball on the full, they immediately throw it up again, calling another country. A player hit by the ball is out after two, three or four hits, depending on the number of players and how soon you want the game to finish.

Selecting teams

An effective way to separate children is to ask them to line up, the tallest at the front the shortest at the back. There may be some minor squabbles, so be prepared to adjudicate. Once the children are in line, it is very easy to send one to one side and one to the other alternately down the line. This method can be used with any number of teams to get them fairly evenly matched.

Beach games

Games make an excellent point of contact with children and families in parks and holiday areas where outreach teams operate. Where beach missions operate the following games are particularly suitable for playing on the sand where a fall is less likely to hurt.

Bundle Race – Ten or a dozen players are bound together with a rope around their waists so that they run as a group. It is more difficult than it sounds, and is generally the occasion of much hilarity when a group crashes.

Chariot Races – Three players kneel on the sand, another two kneel on their backs, while the 'charioteer' kneels on top of them forming a pyramid. To win, a team must reach the winning post without collapsing.

Fighting the Tide – For this game to be successful it is necessary to carefully check the tide charts to ensure that the game is played when the tide is on the rise. A line is drawn along the sand just above where the waves are reaching. On the starting signal, small groups of children begin building a row of sandcastles along this line. When the leader determines that the time is appropriate, the builders place a flag on their castle and stand back to watch as the waves demolish their efforts. The winners are those whose flag collapses last.

Night games

Games played outdoors in the dark are always popular. *Spotto* is a very simple one best played in bushland which has previously been checked for obvious dangers. A lantern is placed in the centre of the playing area. The players' objective is to creep up and turn out the light without being spotted by the 'watchman' who is guarding it. Listening for the sounds of their approach the 'watchman' has a torch which he switches on and points whenever he hears a suspicious rustle. He cannot leave the torch on all the time or sweep the light around. A variation is to have two lanterns at opposite ends of the area. Two opposing teams attempt to be first to extinguish their opponents' light.

Wide games

These games are played over a wide area, preferably rough country.

Storming the Heights – Two opposing teams attempt to smuggle 'flags' into their opponents' base without being captured. Each player has a loop of wool tied above the elbow on the left arm. If this wool is snapped by an opposing player, the player is 'dead' and out of the game until returning to their side's base for a new life.

Coastguards and Smugglers – This is a variation on the above in which the objective is similar but the method of capture is different. In this case, players have a 'life card', with three large letters printed on it, pinned to their backs between the shoulder blades. If an opponent catches sight of the card and calls out the letters, the player must surrender the life card and any 'treasure' that is being carried, and return to their own base to obtain a new life card. Captured life cards and treasure points are totalled at the end of the pre-determined time to decide the winning team. This game has the advantage that the players are banned from manhandling each other so it is better for mixed age/gender groups.

Find the Leaders – works best with younger players. The leaders organise ways that they can merge into the local community for example washing shop windows or disguised as a traveller sitting on a seat at the railway station. The children have to obtain their leaders' signatures to prove they discovered them.

Indoor games

With large groups it is usually better to run games involving a proportion of the children with the rest looking on. This helps in maintaining control but it must be interesting for the spectators. Don't leave them just watching for too long.

Eggs in the Nest – Four circles (nests) are drawn on the floor at the corners of a square and a player stands behind each circle facing seven blocks (eggs) which are placed on the floor in the centre of the playing area. When a signal is given, the players run to the centre of the area, pick up one block each and return it to their circle, returning to the centre for another block. When there are no more blocks in the centre, they can be stolen from other players' nests. This continues until one player has three eggs in their nest. For the next game, another four players are chosen from the spectators.

helping children to trust Jesus

See also ***Metaphors***

When we have opportunities for such significant conversations, we can be so anxious to do it well, that we get tense. The children sense it and they too become nervous.

> It was Saturday morning when two boys knocked at the house where a visiting evangelist was staying.
>
> 'What is it, fellas?' he asked.
>
> They replied, 'About what you said.'
>
> The children who attended the after-school mission had been told that they could come and see him at any time if they wanted to know how to trust Jesus.
>
> They found some seats in the back garden and started to chat about Jesus. After a while the evangelist noticed that they seemed ill at ease and realised for the first time that it must have taken lots of courage for them to seek him out. He consciously let himself relax and casually asked a question about football. After a few minutes talk about footy when he sensed that their nervousness had settled, then led them back to the subject of trusting the Lord Jesus.

For such occasions, choose a location which is away from noise and activities, but not out of sight or secluded, because to do so might cause anxiety in the children and suspicion in their parents. Begin by asking unthreatening questions that require a fuller answer than 'yes' or 'no'.

'Have you ever chatted with someone about how to trust Jesus?'

'What is the thing you most think of when someone mentions Jesus?'

'What made you think of waiting to talk to me?'

Replies to open-ended questions like these give you clues as to what the child is thinking. Sometimes children worry a bit, and may even become visibly upset when they think they don't know the answers. If that happens, make light of it. 'I'm silly. I can see that question is confusing you. Let me ask it another way.'

First steps

When we're helping children to take their first steps of conscious faith in the Lord Jesus, the following steps are essential.

1. Help them see why they need to trust the Lord Jesus.

2. Explain what the Lord Jesus has done for them: dying to forgive them, making them children of God, sending his Spirit to be with them always.

3. Suggest a prayer they can pray to begin trusting the Lord Jesus.

4. Encourage them to keep going and to grow in their faith. A booklet such as Scripture Union's *Starting Out* is helpful.

A valuable resource for talking with children about deciding to follow Jesus is *Team Talk* published by Scripture Union which includes a foldout visual and training handbook as well as a takeaway children's leaflet. Available at www.scriptureunion.org.au.

holiday bible clubs

Planning

Start planning by getting your team together to answer these questions.

What will we call the activity?

What's an appropriate theme on which to focus advertising, decorations, etc?

How many days will it run?

Exactly where will it be held?

For how long will it run each day?

Which age group will we cater for?

What activities will we include?

How many helpers will we need?

Should we impose a charge for those who attend?

Will we advertise through leaflets, posters, banners, local papers, radio spots?

How many leaflets will we need? How will they be designed and distributed? Who will be listed as the contact person?

Who is responsible overall and for each section?

Once these major questions have been answered, the planning moves on to the day-to-day details with another batch of questions.

Bible teaching

How many age sections will be formed? Who will lead them? What is the basic teaching theme? Will the teaching be given by a leader, or by team teaching, or in individual class groups?

Music

Which songs or choruses will reinforce this teaching? Who will provide the music?

Games

What games will suit best? Who will take charge of games?

Refreshments

What should be provided and when? Who will do it?

Craft

Is there time for craft activities? Who will organise them? Will everyone do the same craft? Should there be a different craft project each day? What about a more difficult project that will take the week to complete? (This works better for older children.)

Transport and registrations

How will the children get to the venue and home again? Do we need to make it easier for families to get them there? How will we ensure that we know at all times who is in our care? How will we hand back to carers at the end of each day? What about emergency contacts?

Concluding event

Will we hold a function to conclude the club? What would be the aim of this event? What programme would best meet this aim? What is the best time and place? Who will coordinate it?

Having completed plans for the activity, the group's work still isn't done. Plans need to be put in place for follow-up contacts and activities, like a family barbecue three or four weeks later. While this may appear to be a never-ending story, it is far more effective in the long-term than a series of one-off functions.

Daily programme

By the time you've worked through the questions above, you will have the ideas you need to prioritise your activities and work out your programme. There are a number of possible programmes and each of the books listed at the end of this section is full of excellent programming ideas, but the following chart may also be a useful guide.

Day One will require some time set aside for enrolment, even if you encourage people to register in advance. Plan an activity that occupies those who are already registered and those who are waiting. You may opt for something like games equipment (quoits, skipping ropes, balls), making personalised name badges or painting a mural.

When everyone is together, a good way to start each day's programme is with a **quiz game** (see *Quiz games*). This is usually received with greater enthusiasm by older boys than singing. On the first day, a matching pairs quiz is best because you do not have prior teaching on which to base your questions. On later days, the questions should be based on previous teaching. When a holiday club is a regular annual function, keep in mind that many of the children will be regular attendees, so don't only re-cycle old quizzes.

Daily Programme

Quiz
Songs
Bible memorising
Story time
Small group teaching activities
Games
Refreshments
Craft
Serial story

Singing can follow the opening quiz time. Select songs that will be new to the children.

Part of a **memory verse** could follow at this point. (see *Memorising Bible verses*)

A song or two can precede your **story time**. For the story, vary your presentation. Use flash cards, project-o-graph, quick sketching, drama or another visual approach.

It often works well to have all of the children together to this point but, following the story, separate younger and older children for age-appropriate **Bible activities in small groups**. Doing this gives better opportunity to chat about what they're learning.

Games time for about 30 minutes allows a chance for a change of pace followed by **refreshments**. The snack break can be followed by a **craft** session of about 45 minutes.

For the last 15 minutes of the day it's good to **finish** on a high by reassembling all ages to watch an episode of a serialised puppet play or action drama.

Keep a record of each day's activities so that the following year's programme has enough differences to give the feeling of freshness.

Decoration

The one-off nature of a holiday club lends itself to that something extra that gives the venture the feeling of being special.

One group, uses one of the Narnia stories by CS Lewis each year. The door to the hall is designed as a wardrobe, the hall is decorated with Narnian symbols, the leaders are dressed for the part and a segment of the programme includes a performance of part of that year's story in a serialised form.

Another group in a seaside town had 'Sailing the Sea' as its theme. Every wall in their hall was festooned with nautical symbols: sails, anchors, oars and the like. The Blue Peter was raised on the flagpole in the grounds each morning, and the leaders wore appropriate headgear.

It is not always necessary to decorate to an exotic theme, but when it comes to decorating, the sky (and your imagination) is the limit!

> One country town trucked in sufficient bales of hay to replace the chairs. The main purpose was to create a 'wow' atmosphere for the kids, but it also stimulated adult interest in the activity.

Scripture Union has a variety of theme-based Holiday Club programmes.

Here are just a few

Seaside Rock – Bible stories about Peter with a seaside theme

Xpedition Force – Focus on the cross with a mountain climbing theme

Desert Detectives – The story of the Bible with an archaeology theme

Wet, Wild and Wonderful – Bible stories about water with a watery theme

OnLine: Connecting and communicating with God – with a computer theme

Landlubbers – Based of Philippians with a pirate theme.

icebreakers

See also ***Names***

Here's an idea for getting to know a group of children who are strangers.

Say to a child 'Don't tell me your name. Tell me the first letter'. If the child answers 'S', guess 'Susan, Sarah, Samantha, Shelly, Sausage...Oops...No one ever calls you Sausage, do they?' Carry on in this vein until you discover the right name. By this time, others in the group will be eager for you to guess their names.

Another trick is to guess the children's ages. After you have been doing this a while, you usually come close to the right answer, something that the children find appealing.

Each member of the team should be alerted to the need to be aware of new children, and be prepared to greet them warmly.

> At one Australian beach mission site, the main meeting tent was pitched right beside the path that led to the beach. The team was instructed to be aware of the campers as they passed; perhaps giving a smile, a cheery 'g'day' or making a remark about the weather. It was an obvious point of contact with people, but one sometimes ignored.

In initial contact, clowns can be valuable. They can approach strangers much more easily because they help break down initial hesitancy. Face-painting and balloon twisting are also good ways of making contact.

Pets, especially dogs, are another good conversation starter. It may be difficult to approach strangers to ask their names but, if they have a dog with them, it is easy to ask the name of the dog and thus have a starting point for talking further.

Be aware that wise parents have warned children about strangers, so take steps to overcome their apprehension. Always wear a nametag which clearly identifies who you are and that you are attached to an organisation easily contactable by a parent.

> A beach mission leader invited a boy he met on the beach to come to a holiday programme. The boy replied that his mother wouldn't let him go so the leader suggested that they go together to meet the mother, who willingly gave permission when approached, much to the boy's delight.

illustrating a story

NG A STORY ILLUSTRATING A STORY ILLUSTRATING A STO

Children generally learn more through sight than sound, and they remember stories and characters better than abstract concepts.

This makes pictures a very important addition to storytelling. Drawings capture children's interest and keep them focused. The drawings on the following pages do not require great skill because they are essentially cartoons. Cartoons are simplifications of life, and children and simplicity go well together.

Sketches on paper or card must be large enough to be easily seen by the farthest viewer, so use simple black outlines and a few bold colours. For a large group, the 63 cm by 51 cm card sheets available from newsagents are about the smallest that are practical.

Where to start?

Carefully think about the story. If you are using teaching material, read it thoroughly and reread the story in the Bible. Note the important actions and moods. These are the bases for dividing the story into four or five sections, with a picture for each. Decide whether each section is one of emotion (in which case you may just draw heads)

or of action (when you will draw bodies)

or if it requires both faces and figures. Once you've decided on the emotion or action, take a 2B pencil and soft eraser and make rough sketches of your four or five scenes.

Pre-drawing

In the early stage of your drawing career you will probably want to have the pictures drawn before you go before the group, with any words already on the pictures or on separate pieces of paper or card, ready to attach. Transfer your sketched ideas onto the paper or card at an appropriate scale. Make alterations until you are satisfied, then 'ink in' the outlines with a broad-point, felt-tipped marker pen. Pictures always look better in colour, so fill in the outlines with marker pens or crayons. Clothes can be as colourful as you like, but characters must have the same coloured clothing in every picture to maintain their identities.

For the smooth handling of visuals, mount your drawings on coloured cardboard, perhaps using spray contact adhesive or a removable adhesive so that you can recycle the coloured cards. Try dark blue, grey or cream for sombre moods and red, yellow and bright green for happy scenes. For a small group, one method is to insert your pictures into the right hand sleeves of a refillable display book, but be aware of light being reflected off the plastic sleeves, making it difficult for children to see the picture.

Naturally you will keep your visuals out of sight until you are ready to display them. The expectation of a new and different picture holds attention.

Quick Sketching

Once you feel confident with your drawing abilities, you may choose to take only your sketches with you as a form of notes, and draw directly onto large sheets of paper or a chalkboard as you talk. Some teachers encourage older students to copy the pictures and writing as the story unfolds. If you are of only medium confidence, you can transfer your sketches onto large sheets of paper at home, using a grey chalk pencil, or another tool that leaves lines that you can see, but not the children. You will then be able to trace your drawing in class rather than doing it totally freehand.

Faces

The face is basically an oval which need not even have the features of eyes, nose and mouth, especially in distant figures. The first thing that an infant recognises however, is the face of its chief carer, so it is no surprise that younger children can be upset or non-comprehending of figures with no facial detail.

Eyes are halfway up an adults head, slightly lower in an infant or small child.

The mouth is one third of the distance from the chin to the eyes. Ears basically reach from the eyes to the mouth.

In cartooning, women's eyes tend to be larger, noses smaller and lips more bowed than men's. Old people have longer noses and ears, evil people have smaller eyes closer together, innocents have larger eyes.

Changing the shape and size of facial features not only indicate age, health and sex but, more importantly, attitudes and emotions. For example, there are many forms of happy.

Emotions can be reinforced by eyebrows, especially in the negative emotions.

angry *sad* *worried* *afraid* *blind*

Cartooning is not trying to depict faces as they really appear, but replacing them by a small number of simple symbols. This puts effective drawing in the hands of unskilled artists.

shocked *speaking* *sick/asleep* *lonely* *sorry* *deaf*

Noses play little part in defining a face's emotion, but they do help to distinguish one character from another.

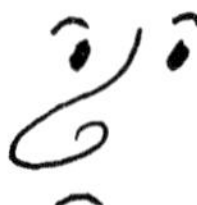 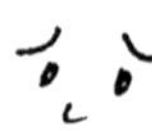     

Beards, ears and hair are like noses; they are decorations which often can be left out because they do not convey emotion or other meanings. Hats, however, have been used by every culture to indicate profession and status; the bigger and fancier the hat, the more important the person.

By combining simple symbols of facial features with symbols for hair, hats and the simplest of decorations, many meaningful characters can be formed.

Stationary bodies

As with faces, bodies have their own stories to tell. We call this 'body language'. Because cartoon figures are simplifications of real life, it pays to compensate by exaggerating the little that you do draw.

For Bible males, start with the 'blob' figure. Make an oval shape for the head but, because more meaning comes from the face than the body, we exaggerate it to be a quarter of the blob's height. Add some downward strokes to form arms and body.

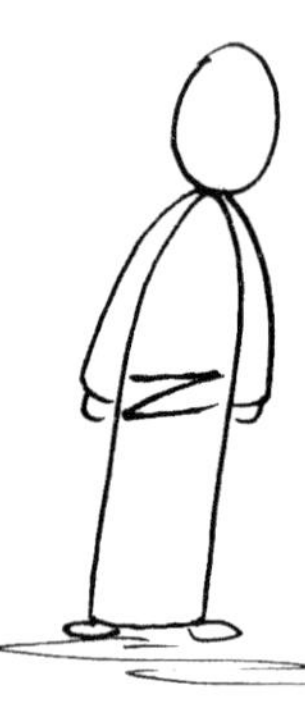

Add curved lines for cuff, hands and feet. A wiggly line underneath makes the shadow that indicates that the figure is standing on the ground or floor.

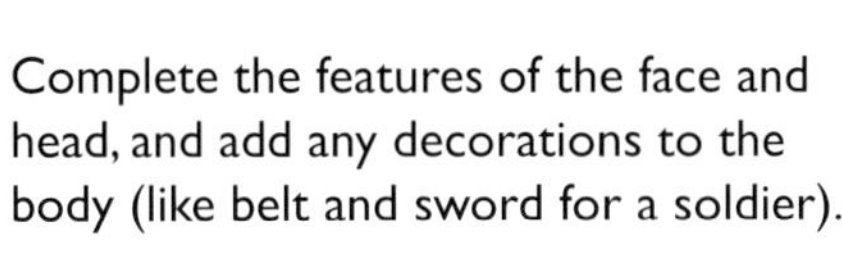

Complete the features of the face and head, and add any decorations to the body (like belt and sword for a soldier).

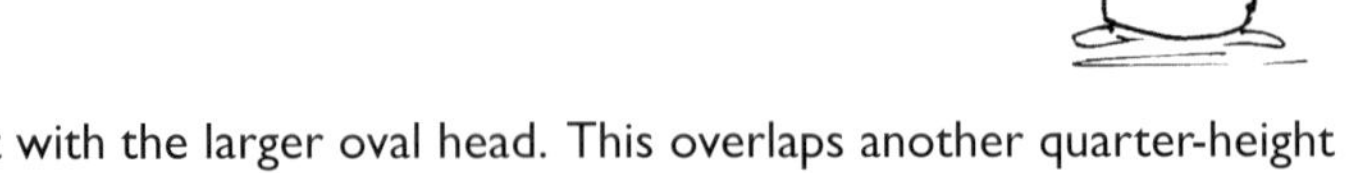

For Bible women, also start with the larger oval head. This overlaps another quarter-height oval for the upper body. The second oval then overlaps a half-height oval.

Add lines for arms, hands and feet. Add the wiggly shadow line to indicate the floor or ground. Now add features of the face and head and any decorations to the body, like a shawl or water pot.

Moving bodies

walking

Try to capture any significant movement in the story by adding actions to your basic body shapes. Some people find it difficult to go from a standing blob figure to the moving blob, so plot your changes by first sketching a stick figure to find the position of the limbs. Because we are drawing cartoons, we compensate for the simplicity of depicting action by exaggerating it.

running

Make the stick figures into blob figures by turning the head, tilting the body to match the speed, and widening the skirt. Follow the figure with speed marks.

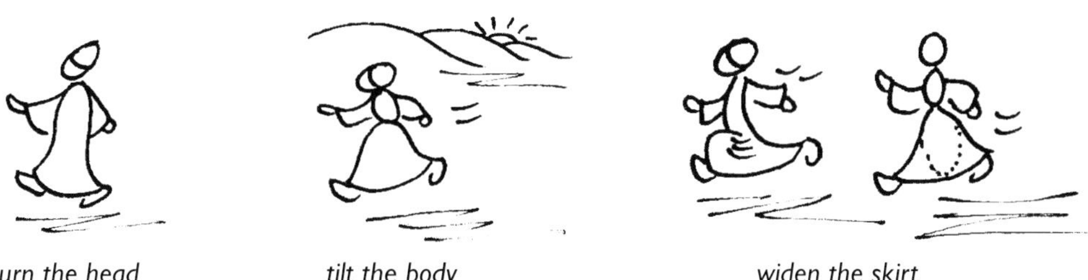

turn the head *tilt the body* *widen the skirt*

Hands and feet

Hands and feet are symbols of secondary importance for conveying meaning except when action is involved. Hands only need to distinguish the thumb from the fingers.

praising or exhorting *speaking or beckoning* *pointing* *making a fist*

Feet are basically ovals which point outwards in front views.

Crowds

Sketch one figure in front, then add circles and strokes for the rest.

Jesus

Some people find it difficult to know how best to portray Jesus and prefer to make most sketches of him from the back view.

Try changing the position of the arms and slightly turning the head for a different angle.

Begin with the head and hair, add shoulders, arms and body, complete with sash.

Scenery

The addition of simple background detail to any picture will help set the scene and put people into context. When working on the chalkboard, draw figures first, then the scenery.

Most outdoor scenes can consist of the same basic outlines. Three hills and a road, river or lake.

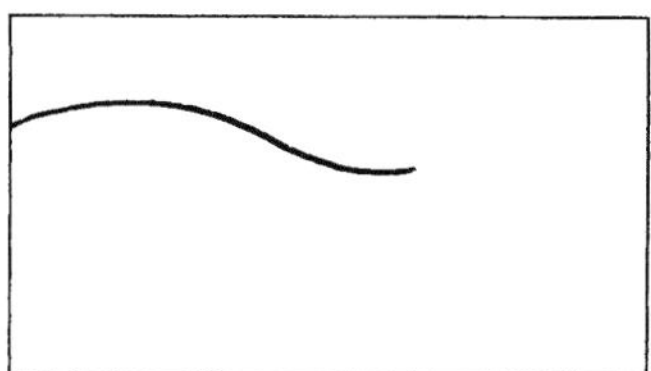

Begin with a curved line which extends halfway across the page.

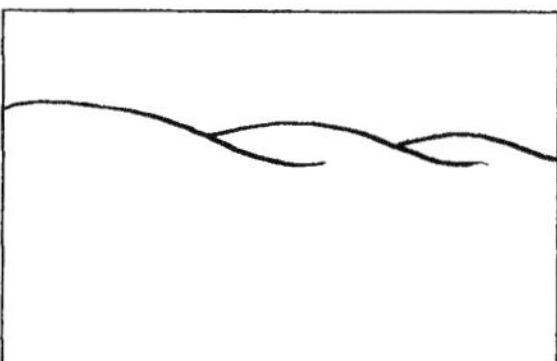

Fill in second and third hills behind and slightly lower.

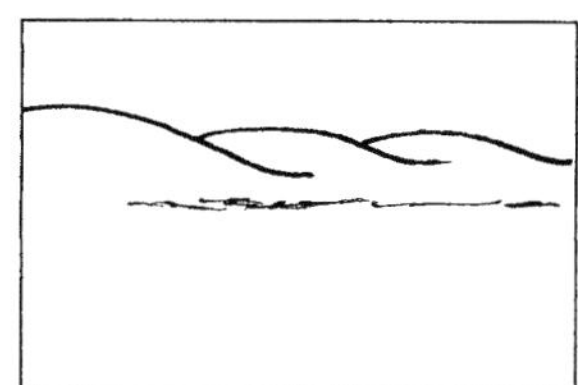

A few strokes across the middle creates distance.

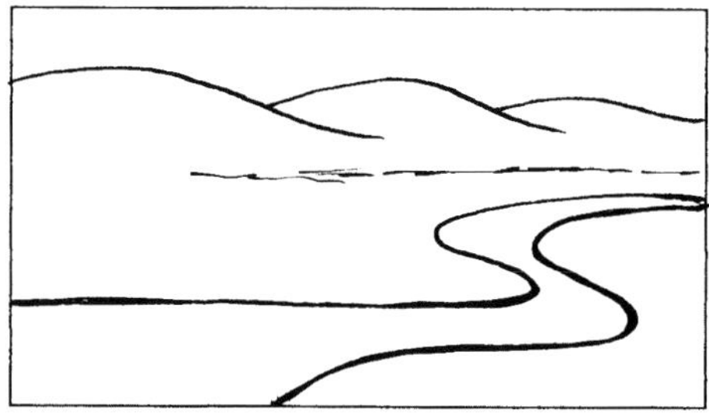

Add two wavy lines becoming wider at the front for a road or river.

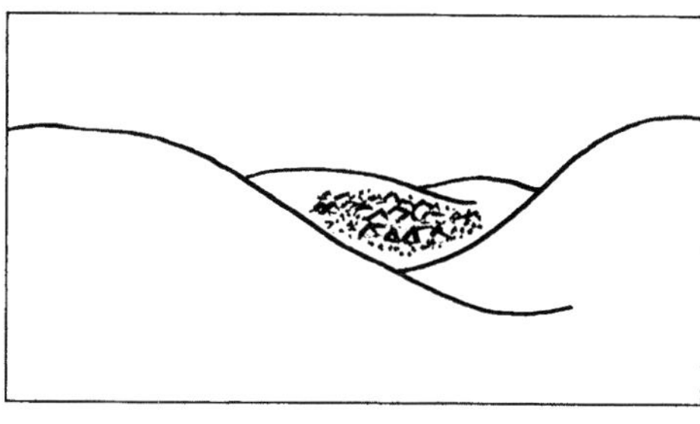

Midianites camped.

Army riding to battle.

Village

House

Road to Emmaus

Palms

Egypt

Trees and bushes

Sheep and goats

Camels

Enemy raiders

Pigs

Lions

Donkeys

Addition of sun or moon can set the time of day

On the sea of Galilee

Jesus calms the storm

Buildings

Perspective is not a problem when sketching scenery but requires a little care when artificial straight lines are significant. In that case, choose a point on the horizon, on or off the sketch, and make all horizontal lines tend to pass through that point. Vertical lines remain vertical.

Tents

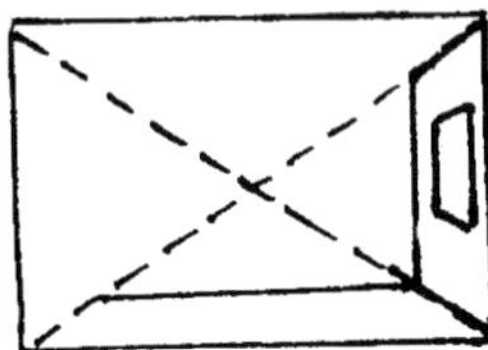

Guideline for interior perspective

Inside house

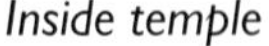

Inside temple

Palace

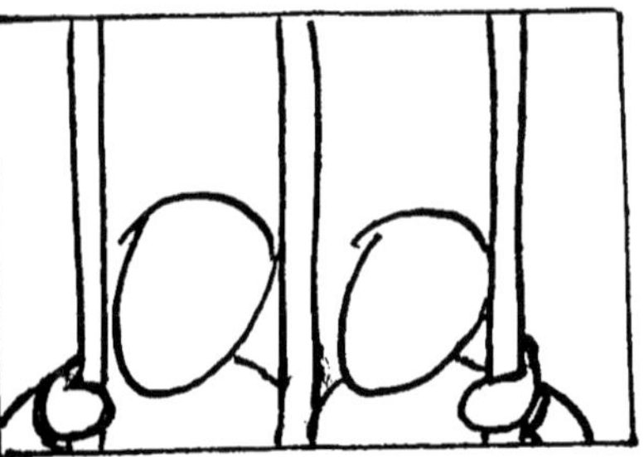

Prison

Angels

Angels can be indicated as different from human figures by adding 'radiance strokes' to the ordinary blob figure.

The Angel Gabriel visits Mary

Blob figure in sitting position

For the angel choir, start with the head oval, add an arm, a hand and robe. To indicate flying/floating, the robe and hair is swept back and feet are not shown and there is no shadow-on-the-ground wiggly line.

Properties

On the stage, properties (props) are small items of scenery that the actors move themselves. In sketching, they are the items in addition to clothing that help identify the characters, like a spear for a soldier. Props, like hats and clothing should stay with the character at all times.

Staff … traveller

Spear … soldier

Crook … shepherd

Bowl … beggar

Children … mother

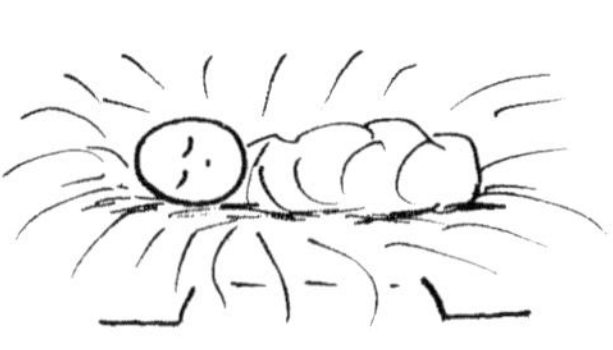

Manger … baby Jesus

Words

Words can help pictures to get the message across. Writing should be in lower case and large enough to be read by the farthest child.

inbetweeners

Children aged 10 to 13 seem so grown up ... *but they're not.* They so desperately want to be teenagers but they're still in our children's programmes, *often under protest!*

Often that's the group of children leaning against a wall muttering under their breath and letting us know in no uncertain terms that they are only with us under sufferance. With all the challenges their involvement can bring, they are an age group with huge potential. They are smart and articulate, aware of the world, aware of their place in it and the impact they can have. They want to make a difference and they believe they can. They are making some huge choices about life, about friends and about faith. Let's look more closely at the characteristics of our 'inbetweeners' and the opportunities we have for ministry to, and with, them.

Characteristics of 10 to 13-year-olds

- **Relationships hold primary importance** and the depth and quality of their friendships can be amazing. They 'do life' together and it is in the context of their relationships that an understanding of the world and a response to it is explored and formulated.

- **Belonging is the driving motivation** as friends become the primary point of reference for this age group. Be aware of the growing emergence of peer pressure and the tremendous influence this can have on their behaviour and attitudes.

- **They want their leaders to be honest and real in their faith and in their world.** They want them to work with them to explore what it means to have faith and to be a follower of Jesus in the world they live in. They are quick to identify leaders who exhibit pretence and hypocrisy.

- **Some activities are almost universal** across this age group. They watch television, listen to music, do homework, hang out with friends, watch videos/DVDs, go to the movies, play computer/electronic games. The upper end of this age group enters the mobile phone market and the whole new language required for SMS communication.

- **Togetherness is key.** They want to have fun and enjoy activities they can do with others in preference to those they can do on their own.

- **Wide possibilities.** They have access to more information and have available to them more opportunities than at any other time in history.

- **Global citizens.** They are developing a strong sense of justice and ask questions about the desperate state of many other children they share the world with. If 11-year-olds were in charge of the world they'd give energy to stamp out poverty and injustice and work hard to stop the spread of HIV/AIDS. The political and historical backgrounds of many of the world's current conflicts make no sense to them – if they've tried to understand them at all. They believe that every child can and should have access to food, water, a safe place to live, education and medical help. There's enough to go around, so why isn't it happening?

- **They enjoy searching for answers.** The questions they are asking are hard, and they revel in the opportunity to explore, evaluate and develop a response. They don't want to learn faith, they need to explore it. They very quickly 'switch off' if they are asked comprehension style questions – particularly those they are confident the teacher already knows the answer to.

- **They are not sure about the future.** They are becoming aware that the world is increasingly becoming a hostile, unwelcoming and unstable and dangerous place.

- **They believe that an individual can make a difference in the world** and in many cases they hope to be that individual.

Sadly, children's workers have sometimes been slow in recognising the unique needs and wonderful opportunities we have for ministry with this age group. Frequently faced with a situation of small groups of children and/or limited available leaders, we have grouped these children in with others, attempting the almost impossible task of selecting a programme and developing activities that will cater for everyone's needs. Even if we select material designed to attract and connect with the 'upper primary age group', the mere involvement of the younger children in the group can see our 10 to13s opting out.

Strategies and activities

Ensure a balance between fun and relevant activities – better still, make your relevant activities fun!

Fun is not only a driving factor for this age group; it's also an attracting one. In working with children we often feel the pressure of 'so little time and so many spiritual truths to impart'. Fun is what they're looking for, relevance keeps them coming.

They want to meet the Jesus who makes sense in their world, a Saviour who came to rescue them and promises them 'life abundant'. Let them explore, share stories, ask questions, draw their own conclusions, make sure you share with them the God who you know, believe in and worship. Your experience of living in this world as a follower of Jesus provides lots of clues for children trying to work it all out in their world for themselves. In following Jesus they will discover real joy, so let your activities be a place where that experience is so evident.

Be proactive about tackling the issues they are facing

Children in this age group are checking out for themselves the relevance of the gospel in their world. They will defend their beliefs with passion and energy, and are carving out for themselves a faith that works. Don't organise activities that see you telling them Bible stories followed by comprehension-type questions asked so you can be sure they've heard. Give them space to ask questions. Be excited, rather than threatened, by the things they desire to know. Encourage them to discover the answer rather than always providing them with one. Jesus made a difference in Bible times and he continues to make a difference today. This difference is what they want to discover. Invite them to a relationship with Jesus and be honest about the impact this will have and the opportunities God has for them to make a difference in the world. The Bible does address the issues of sacrifice, friendship, forgiveness, family, peer pressure, anger and other 'stuff'. Let them explore and respond to this as they refine their grid of reference for understanding and operating in the world around them, discover what they believe and who they want to follow.

Commit to doing life with them

If they want to know what it looks like to be a follower of Jesus, they are going to be watching you. They can't do that if you're on a rotating roster and you get to spend 45 minutes with them once every 6 weeks. Relationships are key with this age group, and not only relationships with each other, but relationships with you. We don't only want to change what they know, our desire is to impact their lives with the person and good news of Christ. You can't do that in 45 minutes and you can't prepare them for a life of living as a disciple in 45 minutes either. Make a commitment to 'do life' with them and show this commitment by giving your time to nurture and disciple them as their developing faith takes on the challenges of their ever-present world.

Empower and equip them for leadership and service

Like all of our children, God has uniquely gifted our 10 to 13s and has a part for them to play in his work in the world. Too often in children's ministry we focus on what we can do *with* them and do *for* them and not what *they can do*. Our 10 to 13s are in a unique position to equip our 6 to 9-year-olds to live as followers of Jesus in their world. After all they have a better understanding of the issues and pressures 6 to 9s face than we ever would. Encourage them to get to know this younger age group, to pray for them and to commit to supporting and developing them. The language this age group uses to explain the good news of the gospel and the realities of living as a follower can be used by God to powerfully impact the lives of younger children. In learning to articulate what they know and experience, we are allowing 10 to 13s to better understand and more confidently express the 'faith they hold within'. Don't forget that with a growing sense of justice comes a growing response of compassion. They believe they can make a difference in the world, they want to make a difference, *so let them.* Let them respond to a world in need with the love and compassion of Jesus. Let them be 'his hands and feet' in their world.

Transition well between children's ministry and youth ministry

Whether we are talking about the transition from primary to high school, high school to the university or from study to work, transition points are times when young people often fall away. How disheartening it is to watch the attendance of children, particularly those you've been working with from your local community, dwindle as they've left children's ministry and started attending youth activities. It's not just the youth ministry's responsibility to 'keep our kids', it's our responsibility to do everything we can to provide a transition pathway which links them from 'belonging' in children's ministry to belonging in youth ministry.

10 to 13-year olds are an awesome age group to work with. Get to know them, find out what they're thinking and where they are at. Embrace their uniqueness, enjoy, empower and equip, don't entertain. Walk beside them as they explore what it means to live a life as a follower of Jesus in a sinful and uncertain world.

intellectually handicapped children

Disabilities and difficulties

Children with an intellectual disability have difficulty learning. The reasons for their condition may be many and complex, but there are often quite specific problems such as impaired sight or hearing, reading difficulties or short attention span. Any generalisations about teaching these children must be modified according to the specific problems in the group. For example, a lot of visual material is generally a good idea, but not if the children are visually impaired. Reading difficulty, however, is very common in this group so when written words are used on diagrams or with pictures they must never be essential to the understanding of the illustration. If all the children in the group are intellectually disabled, use songs that can be learnt by heart. Even if the group has many who can read well, have at least some songs that can easily be learnt by heart.

Age appropriateness

Although some children's intellectual ability may be below that of their age peers, what they are interested in may be similar to others their age. Keep the instructions, the story and the songs simple as you would for a younger child, but recognise that these children have an older interest level.

Teaching techniques

Basic teaching techniques to facilitate attention, understanding and memory are always important if we expect teaching to result in learning, but they are even more important when teaching children with an intellectual difficulty. Therefore, more planning is needed to ensure maximum use of the most appropriate techniques. Gaining and keeping the attention of these children is often difficult. Change activities often to maintain interest. Change the visuals, your voice (tone, volume, pitch, emotion), and your posture. Dramatically change the size or shape of objects used in a presentation. Change from story telling to play acting and back again. Introduce surprises. Stop for a song in the middle of the story if you can find one that fits your point. A puzzling situation helps hold attention, but avoid complex and ambiguous scenarios. Try a little 'horror' and a little conflict in the story and a lot of camaraderie and audience participation throughout.

What will be remembered?

The first thing you say will probably be remembered, so make it significant and make it an attention grabber. The last thing you say is even more likely to be remembered so it should summarise your message. Repetition is an aid to memory and is tolerated by these children more than it is by highly intelligent ones. The verbatim repetition of key words or phrases can bring your audience back to the theme you are developing.

Balance is most important. Have enough of all the good ideas without having too much of any one thing. Too many changes can be confusing. Too much repetition can be boring. Too much conflict can cause withdrawal. Unfortunately getting the right balance only comes with experience, but, if you are conscious of the need for it, it is soon developed.

inviting a response

See also ***Helping children to trust Jesus, Metaphors***

Good manuals on children's evangelism carry strong warnings about the way to invite children to respond to the good news of Jesus.

They advise us to avoid demonstrative methods, and situations that lead to 'copycat' responses. Some evangelists are happy to have an 'altar call' in children's meetings where the boys and girls are invited to come to the front to show that they wish to follow Jesus. Some invite children to raise their hands or stand up, if they wish to 'belong to Jesus' or 'go to heaven'.

The problem with such invitations is that physical response may be just that – a human response to a human calling. We need to be sure that it's the Holy Spirit who is calling for the child's response, and not human manipulation of mind, body and/or emotions.

It's easy to warn people what not to do, but what are some positive steps we can take to help children respond to Jesus? How do we link children who are genuinely open to Jesus with a sensitive, able and pastorally-caring leader who can offer them the help they need?

We can explain to the whole group how they can trust the Lord Jesus, then outline a prayer of acceptance that they can pray at home. If you do this, it is essential to follow it up the next day by giving the children the opportunity for a personal chat, either with yourself or other leaders. That way, you can assess whether they have understood the implications of what they have done, and help them to the next step. The invitation can be given along these lines.

> 'I know that some of you have been thinking very hard about the way the Lord Jesus can be your special friend and Saviour. Yesterday I suggested a prayer that you could pray at home. It was a 'sorry, thank you, please' prayer. Perhaps when you went home, something happened and you were unable to do that. But you can still pray a prayer like that at any time if you want to trust Jesus and give him first place in your life.
>
> 'Some of you may have prayed that prayer last night. If you did, we would like you to stay behind for a short time after we finish so that we can have a chat with you about it.'

It is wise to explain that you intend to finish early to give time for this, and that the other children will be doing something else so they don't think others will go home without them.

Sometimes you may give a talk that is not part of a series, so you will need to provide the children with an opportunity to make an immediate response. As you conclude the meeting, you can say something like this.

> 'After we finish here, everyone will be going outside to play 'poison ball' with Jenny. While that happens, I will be sitting over there (indicate a location – a quiet, public place in view of others). If you have been thinking about putting your trust in the Lord Jesus, you could come and talk to me.'

In this way you offer an alternative to the children so that they have a choice to make, and are not pressured to make a choice they are not ready for.

When you have opportunities for personal conversation, make it brief. Focus on the central issue of who Jesus is and what he has done. To avoid overloading the child with information, it is better to arrange several brief chats rather than trying to cover everything in one long and involved session. You can discuss topics like Bible reading, prayer and telling others in a later conversation.

Having talked with a child about their relationship with God, make it your goal to establish a link between that child and some other Christian or a Christian fellowship so they can be nurtured and established in the faith.

Sometimes we cannot be available for one-on-one chats with the children. In these instances, outline the prayer of commitment that the children can pray at home, then ask them to write a letter telling you what they have done. Arrange for a special letter box where they can 'post' their reply. This approach is not as satisfactory as a face-to-face chat, yet what the children write is often very revealing. When you write back, it is good to pick up something of what they have written in their letter.

In all of the above situations, it is helpful to give some literature. Children can read these on their own, or you can work through them together. Never give the children any hints that you plan to hand out literature or you may find some who go through the process merely to get a free book.

Recommended material from Scripture Union:

For under 8s	*Five things God Wants me to Know/Do* and *Friends with Jesus*
For 8 to 10s	*Team Talk* and *Me+Jesus*
For 10 to 12s	*Jesus=friendshipforever*

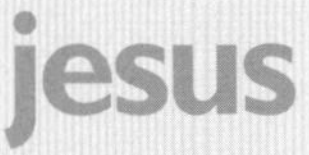

'I believe in God and heaven and all that; it's the stories of Jesus I find hard to accept!'

'I feel the same way', chimed in another in the group of young people. 'These stories might all just be made up by somebody.'

Bible stories such as the virgin birth, Jesus turning water into wine and raising the dead are rightly questioned by children as they get older. On reflection, it is obvious that, if the gospel writers had merely invented stories that they wanted to dress up as fact, they would not have included the miracles. But these writers, claim to have been there or to have talked with eye-witnesses of the events that they recorded, and our faith depends on our assessment of their reliability as witnesses. Here are four tips to help children build an understanding of Jesus as a historical person.

Give attention to historic detail

Watch for the simple details that give incidents from the gospels the ring of reality. Include those details in your sharing. For example, when the conversation between the Lord Jesus and the woman of Samaria was abruptly interrupted by the return of the disciples (John 14:27), she *left her water jar* and hurried back to the city to tell others about Jesus. Obviously, it would be difficult to hurry carrying a water jar, and this statement appears to have no other significance. The mention of the woman leaving her water pot behind gives the account the stamp of authenticity.

On some occasions one of the gospel writers will give some detail that the others miss. Examining all of the accounts of an event gives the fullest possible picture and enables you to discover details you would miss if reading the story in only one gospel. For example, in the accounts of the feeding of the five thousand, Mark is the only one to report that the grass was green and John is the only one to mention the boy with the loaves and fish and to tell us of Philip's protest that eight months' wages would be needed to purchase food for such a large crowd.

Show that Jesus was special

John sums up Jesus' character in the phrase *full of grace and truth* (John 1:14). We must be careful always to depict him in ways that are true to this statement. It seems that one truth that has been successfully communicated to the children in our churches is that the Lord Jesus was sinless. Ask any class of children whether Jesus would ever lie, or cheat, or break a promise, and their answer indicates that this is unthinkable.

It is quite stunning to realise that of all the characters of literature both real and fictitious, only the Lord Jesus is described as morally perfect. No other person has ever faced his critics with the challenge *Can any of you prove me guilty of sin?* (John 8:46) And no-one could.

Report Jesus' emotions

Jesus wept (John 11:35) is the shortest verse in the Bible. More importantly, it helps us recognise that Jesus was truly human.

The gospels record many occasions when Jesus was moved by compassion when confronted with human suffering and need. They also record

- his tiredness as he sleeps in a boat
- his tenderness as he reassures Mary in the garden
- his firmness as he drives the traders from the temple
- his amazement at the centurion's faith
- his distress at the hard-heartedness of those who criticised him for healing on the Sabbath.

Mention reactions to Jesus

As we describe the way Jesus' friends and enemies reacted to him, it helps the children realise that these were real people responding to events that actually took place. When studying incidents, take careful note of the changing emotions. Express them in your tone of voice when you tell the story.

Imagine Philip gabbling excitedly as he approached his friend, Nathanael, *We have found the one Moses wrote about in the Law and about whom the prophets also wrote. Jesus of Nazareth, the son of Joseph* (John 1:45).

Can't you hear the disdain in Nathanael's voice as he sneeringly replies,
Nazareth! Can anything good come from there?

His tone soon changes as he overhears Jesus' remark about him and asks *How do you know me?*

His tone would change yet again as he declares *Rabbi, you are the Son of God, you are the King of Israel.*

It is helpful for young people to realise that even those who were involved were often sceptical until they were confronted by overwhelming evidence. In Luke's account of the resurrection, have you noticed that the disciples did not believe the news that the grave of Jesus was empty? *What the women told them seemed to them like nonsense* (Luke 24:11). Thomas is the prime example of scepticism (John 20:25).

language barriers

See also ***Metaphors***

Much language used in trying to communicate Christian faith is only intelligible to the initiated. We need to work at speaking to children and their families in words and ideas that make sense to them.

Christian jargon

For those who have grown up within the faith it can be quite a challenge to spot the difficulties. Earlier generations of evangelicals were comfortable describing themselves as 'washed in the blood of the Lamb', but to most now, the term seems quaint, and certainly would be a hindrance rather than a help to explaining the faith to outsiders. In the same way, encouraging children to 'give your heart to Jesus' can elicit responses ranging from blank looks to fear. The key is to get to know those we are ministering amongst and their culture, rather than just knowing our message. The younger the group, the greater the necessity of avoiding Christian technical language.

Hymns and songs See also *Singing*

On the first night of one beach mission, the marquee was crowded with both children and adult campers, who had been rounded up by the team.

> 'Let's sing *Great is the Lord*', announced the enthusiastic mission leader.

The team members sang with gusto the song they knew well. The singing was loud enough for the leader to be unaware that the unchurched, of whom there were plenty, did not participate. How could they? They didn't know the tune, and the words were mumbo jumbo to anyone not in the inner circle, and even to many who were, especially children.

Choose songs with words that are meaningful to the audience. Even when jargon is not involved, the wrong words can creep in.

> A 5-year-old was heard singing his own version of a song from *Sound of Music*:
> 'So long, farewell, my feet are saying goodbye!'

When children are older and can read, they may sing the correct words, but still have no understanding of the meaning of those words unless they are encouraged to think about them and, in some cases, have them explained.

Prayer

'We pray that You will undertake for Joe...' A person who didn't know otherwise could be forgiven for assuming we were expecting Joe to die, because that is the time we normally call for the undertaker.

The trouble is that we become more experienced in using and understanding Christian jargon with the passage of time. It is easy to lose sight of the fact that what we are saying may mean something entirely different to others, especially children. With unchurched children, it is probably better even to replace 'Let us pray' with 'We are now going to talk to God for a little while'.

Sometimes the problem may be an experience barrier rather than a language barrier.

> At a family barbecue the organisers were delighted at the numbers of people who never went to church. After the meal the pastor's wife led some singing. 'Let's start with *It's no longer I that liveth, but Christ that liveth in me*' she announced enthusiastically.

The words of this chorus aren't difficult (apart from the seventeenth-century endings) but they express inappropriate concepts for unbelievers to sing.

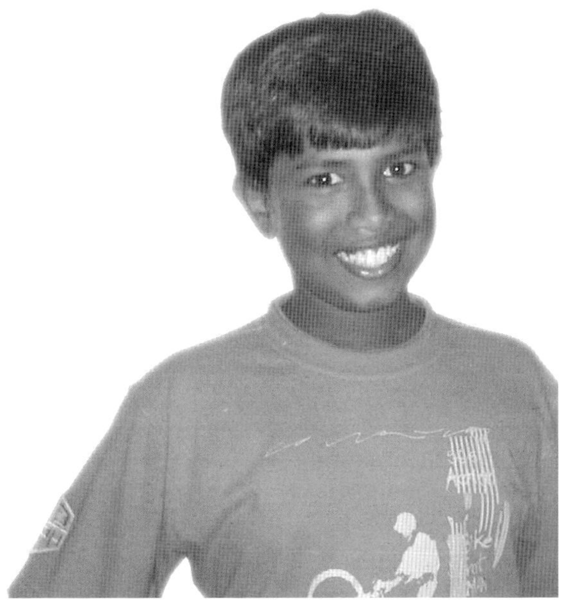

See also ***Design, Writing***

It's no use preparing reading material that people can't read. Whether for children, teens or adults, all reading material must be suitable in letter style, size and spacing.

Children

Don't assume that the children can read what you have written – ask them!
The younger the child, the simpler the style of lettering needs to be.
In their first few years of school, children need larger writing than adults.
Do not 'crowd' your words. Leave adequate spaces between them.
The rules below for adults also apply to children.

Teens

Unusual lettering works well for most teenagers and they are more likely to give your handout a second look if it's just a bit crazy. Beware though; keep the rules for adults in mind.

Adults

Good design is pleasing to the eye and will encourage your reader to look more closely.
If the legibility is low, people will not readily absorb the message, even if they read it.
How many times have you heard someone say 'I didn't really read the church bulletin'?
Is it because they are disinterested (probably not) or too busy (maybe)? Possibly the area of text is too tiring to read.

Top tips to improve legibility

- ALL CAPITALS IS HARDER TO READ than upper and lower case letters. However, for older children, teens and adults, bubble writing and lightning lettering are the exceptions because they can be used for eye-catching effect.
- Underlining is a heritage from the typewriter age and reduces legibility. Instead, use **bold**, *italics* or change of colour for emphasis.
- The longer the length of line the more interline spacing you need – but this takes up space. Imagine a newspaper with lines printed right across the page – impossible to read! So that they can get the maximum of news on a page, the designers divide the page into columns, making it easy to read. Don't be afraid to divide your page into columns with about 40 characters per line (with close interline spacing) to make life easy for your reader! Strangely, legibility drops if there are 20 or fewer characters per line.
- Do not use unfamiliar fonts for areas of text. Keep those decorative letters for headings and titles.

- For large blocks of text use a font with serifs (little feet) like Times Roman. They help the eye follow along the reading line. For subheadings use a sans serif (no feet) font, like Arial, and probably bold.
- Do not use more than 3 different fonts on any one publication. You may have 279 fonts on your computer but resist the urge to use as many as you can on one page! Too many changes are confusing to the eye and reduce legibility.
- Leave space around the page. Space gives a place for the eye to rest and cuts down confusion.
- Dark writing on a light background is easier to read than white writing on a dark background. For example, light blue text on a slightly darker blue background would be hard to read.
- Letters that are too tightly spaced are hard to read – especially for children. Adjust the letter spacing on your computer.
- **Headings need to be bold** with wider spacing to give them importance.

What you want is for your material to stand out from the rest that's out there!

Look at the notices below. The 'weights', sizes and styles of letters vary. There are different amounts of space between and around the words. Which are the most effective? Are any aggressive? Are any hard to read? Which are ineffective? Would you obey their message?

KEEP OFF THE GRASS	KEEP OFF THE GRASS	**KEEP OFF THE GRASS**	KEEP OFF THE GRASS	KEEP OFF THE GRASS
KEEP OFF THE GRASS	**KEEP OFF THE GRASS**	**KEEP OFF THE GRASS**	***KEEP OFF THE GRASS***	**KEEP OFF THE GRASS**

A good talk has a natural flow from one point to the next.

Finding some item that serves as a connecting link can assist cohesion. The talk outline below tells the story of the healing of the paralysed man from Mark 2 using the man's bed (or mat) as the flow-through link.

One day in the life of a bed

Introduction

Discuss how uncomfortable a bed becomes if you are ill. There was a man in Capernaum who could never get out of bed because he was paralysed. His bed was like a prison, he could never leave it.

Start the Bible story

Tell about his friends enthusing about the visit of the Lord Jesus. It must have been very painful to be carried through that crowd. It must have been embarrassing as they struggled to carry his bed up onto the roof of the house. The worst was still to come. Lying on his mat, the man must have been terrified as he dangled through that hole in the roof, hoping the crowd would make enough space on the floor for him to land. When finally the mat hit the floor with a bone-jarring thump, he must have wondered whether it was all worth it.

Looking up from his mat, he could see the faces of his friends peering through the roof. Everyone in the crowd was staring at him. Some looked surprised, others looked annoyed. What would Jesus do? His first words surprised everybody: *Son, your sins are forgiven.*

Life explanation

Explain what sin is. If children are asked, their most common answer is 'doing wrong' whereas it is also 'not doing right' – essentially not trusting our whole lives to Jesus' care (John 3:36 and 1 John 5:12). Remind the group that sin prevents us from living in a way that pleases God.

His friends confidently expected that the Lord Jesus could cure his paralysis. He got much more than he expected – the forgiveness of his sins. Explain that when we ask the Lord Jesus to forgive our sin, we too can confidently expect that he will.

Conclude the Bible story

Knowing that many were critical of him, and to prove that he had the right to forgive sin, Jesus spoke to the man again. He ordered him to pick up his mat and go home. All were astonished when he pushed his way out through the crowd with his mat tucked under his arm. Point out to the children that people believed that a mere man could neither forgive sins nor instantly heal a paralysed person. Jesus healed the man (which everyone could see) so they would know he could forgive sins (which cannot be seen).

That night when the man went to bed he may have looked at that mat and thought to himself 'This mat is no longer my prison. I needn't be frightened of lying down. When I wake up in the morning I'll be able to get up and go wherever I want to. But, Jesus has done something even more wonderful for me. He said that my sins are forgiven.'

memorising bible verses

When teaching children to memorise scripture, aim to teach it so thoroughly that they will be able to recall it for the rest of their lives.

If they can repeat a verse this week but stumble over it a fortnight later, they have not really learned it. Your objective should be that most of the children will know it, not merely the ones with photographic memories.

Repetition is the key

While there are many useful ideas (like puzzle texts and mystery lettering) that make memory work fun, many people make the mistake of spending too much time on the puzzles and insufficient time getting the children to repeat the words. Have the words of the verse on view fairly quickly and spend more time on repetition. Make a game of it, using a variety of techniques like one group repeating it then another group, repeating in a whisper then more loudly, slowly, faster and so on.

A technique that is particularly effective is to focus on a long verse or a short passage and teach a short segment of it each day. Begin at the start of the verse each time it is repeated.

Choosing verses to memorise

Answer these questions when selecting Bible passages for memory work:

- Does the section stand alone, or have you distorted the message by taking it out of its context?
- Have you chosen a translation that makes sense to the children?
- Are there any difficult words or ideas that should be explained?
- How will you help the children to discover the application of the Bible truth in their lives?

Suggested verses and passages

Verses that aid understanding of who Jesus is
(The 'I am' verses) John 6:35; 8:12; 10:11; 11:25; 14:6; 15:5.

While these verses have been popular, they focus on the abstract and will need explanation. A longer passage in this category is Philippians 2:5-11.

Verses that show the benefits of having faith
John 1:12; 1:16; 3:16; 5:24; Acts 4:14; Romans 6:23; 10:9; 1 Timothy 1:15.

Verses that give assurance
Isaiah 30:21; Psalm 48:14; John 16:13; 1 Corinthians 10:13; Hebrews 13:5; 1 Peter 5:7.

Verses that give instruction for life
Philippians 4:8; Colossians 3:9; 1 Thessalonians 5:15.

Verses that show the value of the Bible
Psalm 119:105; 119:18; 2 Timothy 3:16; 1 Peter 2:2; 2 Peter 1:16.

Verses that help understand doctrine
Romans 3:10-11; 3:23; 5:6-8; 6:23; 8:38-39; 12:1-2.

Longer passages
Exodus 20:1-7 (the Ten Commandments); Matthew 6:9-13 (the Lord's prayer); 1 Corinthians 13; Psalms 23; 100; 121; 150; James 1:23-25; 1 John 1:5-7; Ephesians 6:11-18; Isaiah 53:5-6; 55:6-7; 1 John 4:7-12; Matthew 22:37-39; John 14:1-6; Matthew 5:3-12; Proverbs 3:5-7.

Memory verse ideas

While sounding a caution not to let the visual presentation take time away from the repetition of the verse, making your presentation fun will aid the learning process. A favourite is to print the words on each side of a large carton and spin the box, reading the words as they are revealed. When everyone has repeated the words three or four times, a child can be chosen to try to spin the box in the right order. The illustration demonstrates the sequence for marking the box. (Notice that the words on the sixth side are upside down to those on side three.)

- Print the words on cards cut to the shapes of clothing which are pegged up on a 'clothesline'
- Hide the words on slips of paper in inflated balloons
- Print the words on paper aeroplanes which are brought to the front by the children who catch them

- Glue words to footballs which can be thrown to the audience
- Hide the individual words in a defined area. As they are found, display them.
- Write the words on the side of large boxes or wastepaper bins.
  Challenge children to throw a ball or sponge into the correct boxes in order.
- Use an overhead projector to display the whole verse. Rub of one word at a time, getting the group to repeat the verse until no part of it is on display.

metaphors

See also ***Language barriers***

Children have difficulty in dealing with metaphors and figurative language, so we need to be careful.

> A mother was speaking to her 8-year-old daughter about asking Jesus to 'come into her heart'. Her thoughtful 4-year-old interrupted with a serious question: 'What happens to Jesus when the food goes down?'

In helping children to start a new life with Jesus, rather than use metaphors, encourage them to use three straightforward ideas in a prayer: sorry, thank you and please.

I'm ***sorry*** for my sin.
Thank you for dying on the cross for me.
Please forgive me and be my Saviour!

Avoiding figurative language poses problems with theological concepts like 'sin' and Saviour. These are not everyday words and their meaning can be difficult to grasp. However, when used with care, biblical metaphors will serve our teaching. Why? Because a picture is worth many words. Take, for example, Jesus' statement, *I am the light of the world.* We can explain that the light from a torch can show us the way to a destination and Jesus, like that beam of light, is the way. God the Father is the destination (John 14:6).

Take care to explain the picture the metaphor paints in concrete terms (see *Abstract Ideas*) and then make the connection with what is meant by the text. If we wish to encourage children to read the Bible, we must be ready to teach the meaning of biblical terms, phrases and expressions.

A helpful book on this subject is *A-Z of Communicating Christian Concepts* by Owen Shelley, published by Scripture Union in 2005.

See also ***Icebreakers***

You may need to ask some children a number of times before being able to commit their names to memory.

Perhaps you only meet them once a week in a large class or kids' club. It's possible to carry on each week without taking the trouble to learn their names, but it's not desirable. Knowing a person's name is an important step in establishing a relationship.

In our multicultural society, some names may be difficult for us, but we must make the effort to learn these names correctly. It may seem funny to us if we think a name is unpronounceable – but it isn't to the child. Asking children to spell their names for us can help our memory. Never make fun of a child's name. It may be tempting to make a joke if a boy is called 'Angel' or 'Hercules', but resist that temptation.

Use nametags

The first time you meet your group it's a good idea to make personalised name tags which allow you all to share something about yourselves.

For a classroom situation, use a folded piece of cardboard on which the child's name is easily seen. Simply place the folded card on the child's table or desk. (Beware, sometimes children switch cards.) An A4 sheet of paper folded in thirds will stand by itself and can be unfolded to slip into a plastic sleeve for you to take home at the end of the session, or children can keep theirs in their workbook, to be on hand for the next session.

Keep a class list and make notes to help you match the names to the children. Test yourself at home until you know everyone's name.

One way of learning names

Have an OHP transparency with an illustration of some kind and the word 'Welcome' on it. Ask the children to put up their hands if their name starts with the letter A and, as they reply, write them on the transparency with a temporary pen. After about ten or a dozen, pause and say 'Let me see if I can remember who belongs to these names.' Then point out each child in turn.

At any one session don't attempt to record too many names. In a large group, choose a few letters at random each day. Once you have learnt a name, use it repeatedly in that session to help cement it in your memory. This is important in being able to recall the child's name the next time you meet.

opening the bible with children

The Bible has been compared to a treasure chest with jewels waiting to be discovered. Some have also likened it to a maze or a darkened building through which children are trying to find their way. Is it any wonder that we need sensitivity when we open the Bible with children?

Key considerations

Enjoy

Opening the Bible with children has to be fun. It should involve making new discoveries and being challenged. It should never, ever be boring.

Engage

Seek to offer a wide variety of activities, not simply exercises in reading and/or comprehension.

Point to the author

Sometimes we put so much energy into looking at the text that we neglect to allow children to discover for themselves through the text what God is saying or doing.

Explain and practise

The way the Bible is 'put together' needs to be explained. Finding the books and passages, working with references and the contents and index needs to be practised until mastered.

Interpret

As children develop, their interpretation of a text will change. We must value the interpretation they have at the moment, but sensitively coach them into a fuller understanding. A good Bible coach will develop an understanding that says 'We are in this together. Let's share the meaning we both discover.'

> A 7-year-old, when asked what happens when we ask God to forgive us, replied 'It's when God says "that's OK, it doesn't matter any more."'

Helping children discover meaning

Asking questions is one way of allowing children to discover the meaning and implications of a story or passage. Terry Clutterham in *The Adventure Begins* sets out five excellent questions to use.

> What is God like?
> What has God done or what is he doing or what will he do?
> What does God want?
> What does God not want?
> What might it be like to live with this God?

Some extra questions could be

> What might it be like to know this God?
> What do you like most about this passage?
> What do you think is the most important bit?

Obviously not all the questions will be asked at one time, and they could be asked in any order. The questions are for leaders to have in mind and could be written on a bookmark in your Bible. They are not to give to the children. By asking any one of these questions and providing supportive coaching, you may be surprised by the discoveries children make.

> One 9-year-old, when asked 'What might it be like to live with this God?' answered 'It will be great days, no horrible days and you won't want to do bad things.'

overhead projectors

See also ***Project-o-graph***

Exciting new opportunities have opened up with the use of electronic visual presentations, but the humble overhead projector (OHP) is still a valuable tool. It works well, is affordable, and holds a number of possibilities that most people have yet to try.

Top tips for using the OHP

- Align the light produced by the OHP and the screen so that both are as close to square as possible.
- Understand the buttons and focus mechanism for the OHP you're using.
- Leave yourself plenty of time before the audience arrives to position and focus the OHP.
- If your screen has a keystone eliminator which tilts the top of the screen forward, use it!
- The closer the OHP is to the screen, the smaller the image. Spend some time playing with image size that suits the size of the audience.
- Make sure no direct sunlight hits the screen.

Guidelines for effective OHP transparencies (acetates)

Maximise the letter size

Make 36 point your minimum size - the equivalent of 12.5 mm (half an inch).

Minimise the content

Don't cram too much material onto each transparency. Books on OHPs recommend six to eight words per line and six to eight lines per visual. While this may be too limiting for songs or hymns, it's a good guide. Never cram two songs onto one transparency. If the song is a short one, make the lettering larger, centre it and spread it out. Use an uncomplicated, sans serif font like Arial, in lower case with the minimum of capitals.

Enliven with colour

While black shows up best, especially if you intend to use the material in daylight, you can use colour in a variety of ways to give your presentation a lift. Words are much more interesting if accompanied by a colourful illustration. Transparencies can be coloured in with overhead projector pens. Use permanent pens, not those labelled 'temporary', which smudge.

Create interest with pictures

A transparency can be produced with a plain paper photocopier using the special transparencies that have been developed for this purpose. Place your paper master under the lid and the transparency in the paper feed, and press the button. You can add illustrations clipped from various sources to your paper master before you copy it.

Additional uses of the OHP

Wipe off

A dramatic effect can be achieved by wiping off text that is written with non-permanent (water-soluble) pens. For example, the words of Thomas found in John 20:25 are *I will not believe*. The word 'not' could be written with a water-soluble pen, the other words with a permanent pen. As you describe his confrontation with the risen Lord, you can wipe out the '*not*' leaving *I will believe*.

Shadow puppets

Place your figures directly onto the lit area of the OHP to form silhouettes.

Enlargements

Large posters, backdrops and banners are easy to make with an OHP. Find an uncomplicated piece of artwork, which could include lettering. (Make sure you abide by copyright rules.) Print the artwork onto a transparency. Place a large sheet of paper, cardboard, fabric (calico) or even white-undercoated plywood onto a wall. Project the illustration or text onto this material and draw around the enlarged image in pencil. Add colour, then stand back and be impressed!

Overlays

This involves placing one transparency on top of another to add text, colour or content to the first. Two further transparencies can be used but more than four layers will affect the brightness of the image. Attach the first transparency to a frame and hinge the others with tape so that, when moved in, they stay in the right position.

Frames can be cut from cardboard, the dimensions being 34 cm x 26 cm with a piece measuring 25 cm x 20 cm removed from the centre. Some cleverly artistic people have made interesting additions by cutting designs into the edging frame.

Backdrops

A projected illustration that accompanies a Bible passage, which is being read aloud, is very effective. Have one or two images only, because too many can cause people to concentrate on seeing rather than hearing .

Computer-created OHP transparencies

By using a drawing program on your computer, a colour printer, scanner and compatible transparency film, you can create spectacular transparencies. It's essential to use the correct film for your brand and type of printer. Here are a few tips for starters:

- Use cool colours for backgrounds.
- Centre headings and left justify other pieces of text.
- Avoid strong reds for lettering.
- Add a scanned picture or cartoon whenever possible.
- More is not always better. Think how roadside billboards are designed.
- Landscape page set up makes for easier viewing.
- Attach the transparency to a cardboard frame. (This prevents unwanted light from the projector spoiling the effect.)

participation

PARTICIPATION PARTICIPATION PARTICIPATION PARTICIPA

Children like to be part of the action, so involve them in what you do whenever possible.

Ideas for involving individuals

The simplest form of involvement is to be asked to 'help'. For example, many children are familiar with the overhead projector and can change transparencies for you, others can connect up and operate the CD/DVD player or TV. Even those who express confidence should be asked to demonstrate the necessary skills with your materials before being entrusted to operate the equipment in a session.

Children enjoy being chosen to be 'captains'. If you run an overhead projector quiz game for instance, choose two captains to move the markers representing their teams on the screen.

Choose children to hold up song cards, to lead the actions for an action song, or to respond in a conversation with a puppet. Older children could help as puppeteers, provided there is time available for them to practise with you beforehand. Use your imagination, accepting offers of help whenever it will benefit all concerned.

When a 'helper' isn't helpful

While most children enjoy participating, some become self-conscious or attention-seeking when out in front and, as a result, they can become a hindrance rather than a help. When this happens, for example when a child deliberately holds a card upside down, act calmly and decisively, either making light of it, taking the card away and signalling the child to return to his place without comment, or saying 'I'm sorry, but I don't think you can be sensible enough today, perhaps I'll pick you again tomorrow.' Never resort to ridicule or show your irritation by making a cutting remark. Such actions only serve to put a barrier between you and the child concerned. If you find it necessary to correct children in front of others, make an opportunity to relate positively to them at a later time so that it is clear that you have no continuing animosity. It is wisest not to refer back to the incident because this may give the impression that you are apologising for being firm.

planning / preparation

See also ***Classroom management***

Many of us are guilty of planning 'on the run' and wonder why our programme fails to appeal. Whatever the activity – holiday club, after-school club, Sunday School, beach mission – thoughtful planning and thorough preparation are essential for successful ministry.

It's generally worth running fewer sessions and using the extra time for planning. For example, a weekly club could operate only in term time, with the term breaks being used for leader preparation.

> An excellent children's Sunday group was led by a man who left nothing to chance. He recorded in a notebook the name of the teacher he had asked to be responsible for the offering the following week. At the appropriate moment he would announce 'We will now have our offering', and the appointed teacher would come forward with two children whom the teacher had chosen for the privilege. The teacher passed the plates to these children who took them around the group. On completion of their round, they returned to the front where their teacher led the dedicatory prayer, and the three then returned to their places. What a contrast between this planned approach and the way it is done in most groups!
>
> Another of his innovations was to use the small groups with their leader to contribute an item of lesson revision each week in the opening together time. This was organised two weeks ahead, giving the class leader a week to plan the class' contribution, and a week to practice before their turn came to participate.

prayer

Some people treat prayer as a ritual that must be performed at the commencement and the conclusion of every meeting.

Have you ever been an embarrassed observer as a leader struggles to gain control of a group of children to lead a closing prayer? 'We're going to stay here until you are quiet', the leader thunders. After a series of threats, the children do become quiet and the leader manages to mumble a prayer, usually one in which the children have no interest or sense of participation.

In preference to ranting at the children to be quiet so that you can pray, it may be best to do your praying privately. Alternatively, you could ask the children to repeat phrases of an appropriate prayer after you. This often works with younger children, but older ones generally do not engage with this approach. If you use responsive prayer of this type, you need to prepare what you intend to say beforehand, perhaps even write it out. The prayer of the unprepared leader often begins with short phrases that become longer and more complex as the prayer progresses.

One positive approach is to ask the group beforehand for their suggestions of things to pray about. And, yes, it is OK to write out public prayers beforehand so you do not fall into some of the above traps. Written prayers are no less spiritual than extempore prayers.

Top tips for public prayer with children

- be brief
- don't preach a sermon
- don't use a special voice
- use respectful everyday language.

Children praying themselves

Helping children learn to pray is a long-term project in which teachers and parents all have a part to play.

There are numerous biblical examples we can use to teach the importance of prayer but it is only as we put prayer into practice that we can expect the children to learn how to talk with God themselves.

Recording requests and answers can help prayer to seem more effective and real. When praying with your class or even with your own family, ask them what they feel they want to ask God about, rather than imposing your own ideas. Help the children to see that thanking God is as important as asking for something.

While prayer in your class or group will be quite normal, your objective is for the children to develop to the point where they pray alone. As their teacher, thoroughly familiarise yourself with passages such as Matthew 6:5-14 to give a firm biblical basis for your teaching.

problems

One of the statistics recorded in international tennis matches is 'unforced errors.' These suggest that the players only have themselves to blame for losing these points. In ministry there are a number of errors to grapple with.

Failure to check thoroughly

Make a checklist and use it before you leave home so you are confident that you have everything you need.

Failure in maintenance

If you are expecting to use someone else's equipment you will need to check it in advance.

Problems still occur with the gear you use fairly frequently. A loose wire in an amplifier can cause panic if it's discovered just as an assembly is about to start. Carry a small screwdriver, all purpose tape and some pliers as part of your kit – and know how to use them.

Failure to practise

Those using data projectors need to be well practised in computer use so that, if an incorrect key is pressed, fast recovery is possible. An adult audience will sit politely while the problem is sorted out, but a group of children will quickly become restless. Practice will help to avoid this muddle.

When someone else is operating the controls while you speak, it's important to clarify beforehand what you both expect. Problems often occur when the operator fails to concentrate, no longer synchronises with the speaker and then hurriedly tries to catch up. Practising beforehand with your assistant can help to sharpen your presentation.

project-o-graph

PROJECT-O-GRAPH PROJECT-O-GRAPH PROJECT-O-GRAPH

With a project-o-graph, the background picture is projected with an overhead projector and the figures of the characters involved are added as the story unfolds.

These figures can be either cardboard cutouts which will appear as silhouettes, or figures printed on transparencies. In either case, the figures should be hinged to the frame so that they can only move in and out of one position.

The illustrations here can be used to present the story of the crucifixion according to John's gospel. Enlarge and copy them onto two transparencies. Cut the overlay into strips and hinge the people to the bottom of the frame and the writing to the top in such a way that they fit the spaces between the crosses and the sponge and the spear reach the right points.

It is finished

See also ***Colour, Design***

For publicity to be read in these days of information overload, it must contain essential details only.

The aim is to inform, enthuse, and invite. A poster or leaflet is more effective if the design is good. People are bombarded with well-designed information from TV, cinema, newspapers and advertising leaflets. We have to compete for attention, so spend extra time on your planning to achieve professional-looking promotion material.

Planning your publicity

- **Determine the target audience**
  The style should be determined by the target audience. If it's parents, don't be flippant. For teenagers, keep it light and friendly. For children, use easy words with simple lettering.

- **Gather the information**
  Follow the 4WH principle – Answer the questions What? Who? When? Where? How? (how much? how do I get there?)
  Make sure your publicity includes everything the audience needs to know.
  Decide which bits of information are most important.

- **Think of an 'attention grabber'**
  This must connect with your particular target audience. A good attention grabber will draw the right people to take notice with something eye-catching, like an appropriate illustration, arrows or colour.

- **Decide where it will be used**
  Will it be displayed in a large hall? At the end of a corridor? A small room? In the hand? Outside? On a public notice board? All these things determine the best size and colour.

Layout and design

- **Size**
  If a poster is to be viewed from a distance, it must be large and the lettering needs to be big and heavy, extra bold. It also needs more space between the letters than normal. (On a computer, use the character spacing option.) For a hand-held leaflet, the letters can be lighter weight.

- **Ordering of information**
  The most important words must be the largest and heaviest and could be in a decorative font (letter shape). The rest of the information will go down in size, relative to its importance. Use a simple font for less important information. Never use more than three fonts or scripts. In fact two is often better as it gives a less cluttered look.

- **Colour**
  Colour will add interest to your promotions but it can be more expensive, so plan carefully.

Display

If a poster or handout needs to be displayed for a long time, particularly outdoors, consider what it will look like after a week or two, or after a day of rainy or windy weather. Bubble jet printing will 'bleed' if it gets wet. This can be prevented to a large extent by spraying the work with 'workable fixative' (available from art shops). For a more permanent finish, have the work laminated, at a large office supply store or copy shop.

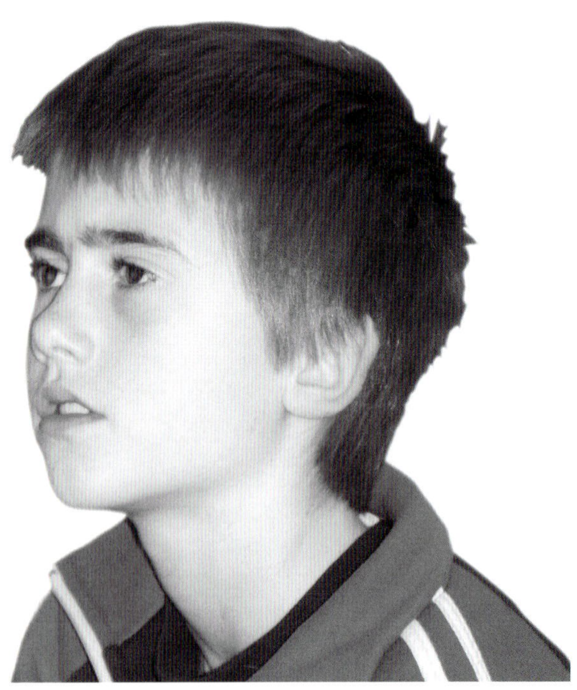

puppetry

Puppets are very popular with children and, because they prefer concrete thinking, children grasp issues better through visuals like puppets than through words alone.

Puppets work well for adults too. Many who would find it too threatening to go to a children's talk are happy to attend a puppet show. People of all ages enjoy seeing characters struggling with life and finding ways to overcome their problems.

The puppets commonly in use in children's ministry are glove puppets, shadow puppets and mouth-opening puppets

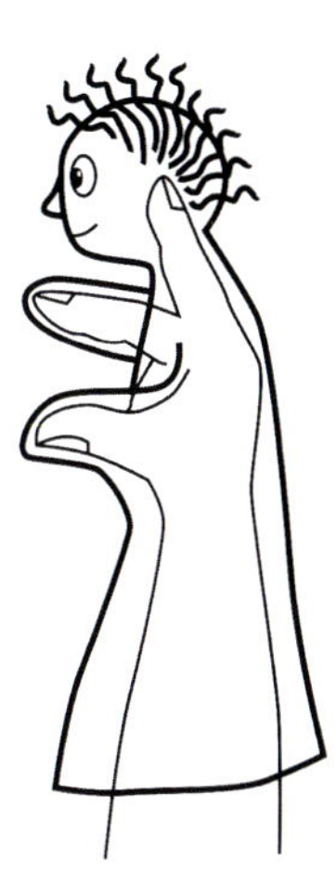

Glove Puppets

Make your own glove puppet

For an easy method of making the head, use a 75 mm diameter polystyrene ball available from craft shops. Pin on a small polystyrene nose and insert 20 mm diameter uPVC electrical conduit for the neck. Stretch a 20 cm square of flesh-coloured, double-knit interlock cotton stretch fabric over the face and glue with PVA glue at the back. PVA-glue two 12 mm joggle eyes (from craft shops) and a strip of felt for a mouth. On men with beards, a gap in the beard replaces the mouth. Hair can be ignored for Bible characters with headdresses, otherwise use bunches or yarn or fur fabric.

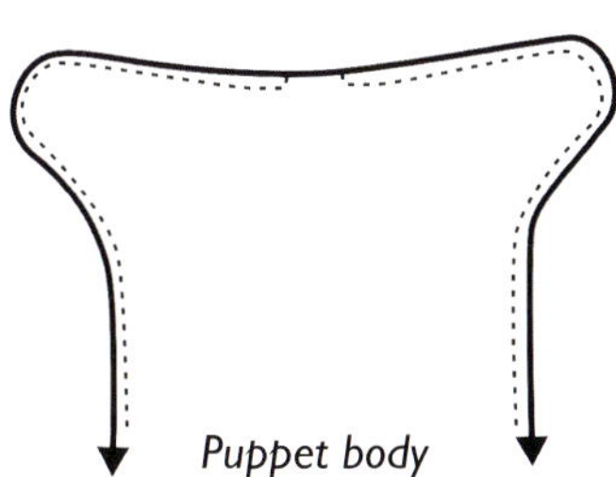

Puppet body

The puppet body is cut from two 40 by 40 cm pieces of stretch fabric. Arms are enough of a symbol to indicate a human figure, and the absence of hands makes it easier to handle props in a believable fashion. After sewing and turning inside out, the body is PVA-glued to the neck.

Cut clothing from two 38 cm by 19 cm pieces of knit fabric. Sew the sides and turn right-side out, then oversewn at each shoulder into the body, close to the neck.

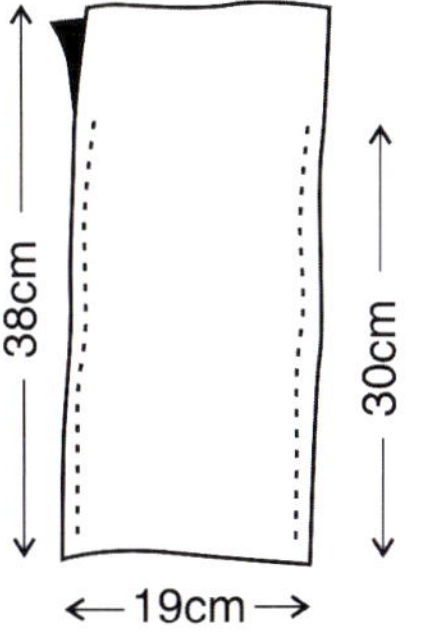

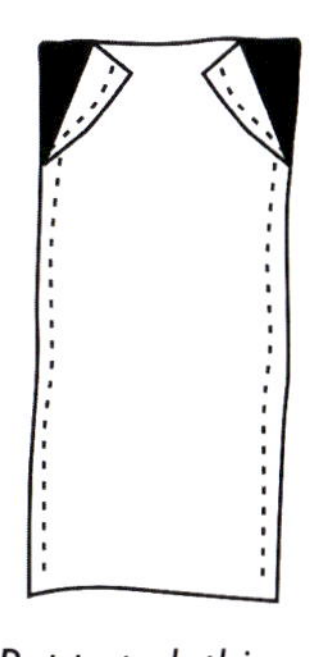

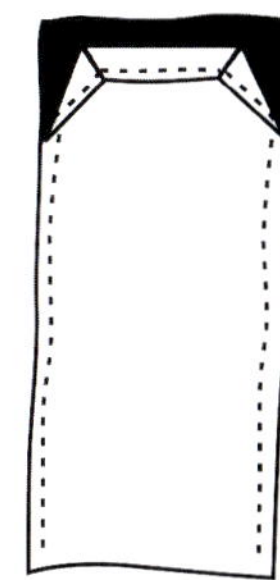

Puppet clothing

Use purple fabric for royalty, light blue for the Virgin Mary, small floral and prints for Bible females and plain colours or stripes for the males. Add simple extra symbols such as neck medallions for important people, holed hessian for beggars and a belt and shoulder strap for soldiers. Like a cartoon, a puppet should contain the minimum number of symbols necessary to convey the character.

A glove puppet theatre

Not all glove puppeteers use a theatre but many prefer it. A 'theatre' can be a table, a piano top, a curtained-off doorway, or even an old refrigerator carton, but a light, transportable purpose-built theatre becomes economical for more frequent puppetry.

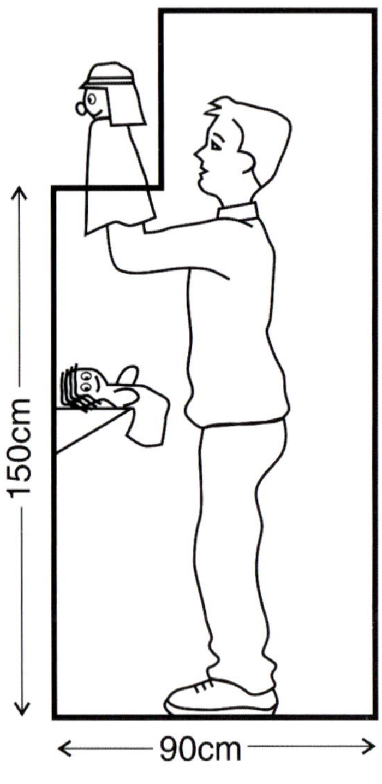

Your theatre should be tall enough for the puppeteer to stand upright and be comfortable. Include a **shelf** inside for puppets and props with a towel across it to limit noise when objects are put down or dropped.

A **backdrop** of see-through, plain dark-blue fabric allows the puppeteers to see their puppets without being seen by the audience. If you have more complex or painted backdrops make sure the puppets stand out against them.

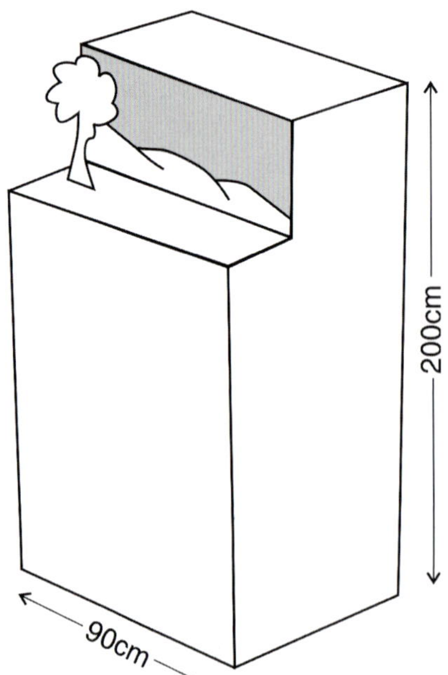

Lighting Focus attention on the stage with two lights shining down at 45° from 45° left and right of centre stage (to wash out each other's shadows). Use mirror-backed 75 W lamps, with shades to prevent distracting glare.

Make simple, symbolic **scenery** from corrugated cardboard or 3 mm plywood. Use only one major and perhaps one minor item. For example, three low hills across back of the stage (major item) and a tree at the front of the stage for the

robbers to hide behind (minor item). Working scenery changes into the script or using an elbow-length blue gloved hand or a special 'roadie' puppet eliminates the need for a curtain.

Puppet theatre backdrops

Pre-recording scripts

Pre-recording of scripts allows the use of interesting sound effects and frees up puppeteers to concentrate on movement rather than reading or memorising voice parts. Use a good quality player and an amplification system, if possible. When you check the sound beforehand, remember that during the performance sound will be deadened by the audience.

Top tips for working with glove puppets

- Practise so that the puppets act naturally and don't gaze at the floor or the ceiling.
- Talking puppets move their arms and head slightly in time with the syllables, rather than shaking their whole body from side to side. Non-talking puppets are held still.
- Conversing puppets should face halfway between the audience and each other.

- Avoid vertical entrances and exits.
- Puppet people walk with a bounce, a twist and a swinging arm rather than sliding.
- Combine body and arm movements (like bouncing up and down while clapping with joy) to accentuate actions.
- A puppet can go to sleep by first lying down facing the audience, yawning, breathing twice, then turning over so its back is to audience.
- Use hook-and-loop tape (Velcro® or similar) to fix props to the puppets' hands. White tape can be tinted with marker pens to blend in.
- Don't use a puppet whose character is known to your audience from other sources. You could be infringing copyright and will probably disappoint or offend your audience because you cannot match the voices, personalities and production techniques of the media originals.

Shadow puppets

Shadow puppets are 2-dimensional figures moved with a wire across a translucent sheet of material which is lit from behind. Shadow puppetry allows for lots of imagination, the use of symbols and spelled-out words.

Because dialogue is less convincing in shadow puppetry, scripts often are ones in which a narrator tells a story which is acted out by the puppets. Bible readings, usually modified with suitable additions, omissions, and pauses, make excellent shadow puppet scripts.

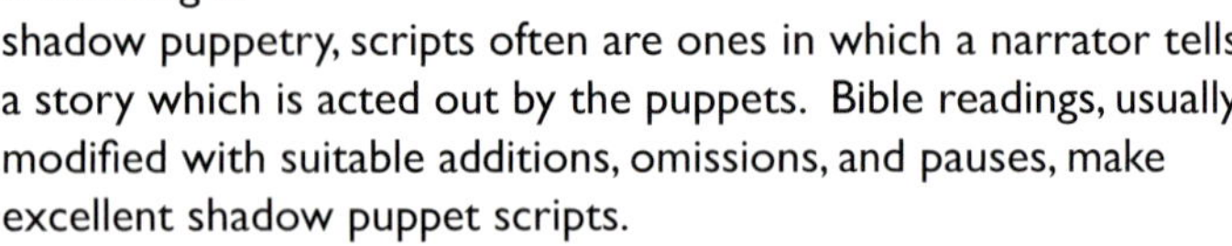

Make your own shadow puppets

Thin black cardboard is adequate. Books like *How to Cheat at Visual Aids*, Scripture Union, provide a source of characters for enlarging or reducing on a photocopier. Cut-outs may be filled with cellophane for coloured effects.

Joint one or two body parts using a paper fastener covered with masking tape to prevent light passing through the hole and to prevent tangles with other puppets. With tape, hinge a long wire ('control rod') to the upper portion of the puppet back.

Making the shadow puppet theatre

Screens can be

- light translucent material fitted to a regular puppet theatre.
- white cotton stretched across a rectangular wooden frame in the ratio of about 2 high to 3 wide with corrugated cardboard or plywood wings hinged to each side to stop light 'spill'.
- made from a 1220 mm by 905 mm sheet of 3 mm plywood or MDF cut into four pieces as shown with an A2 sheet of drafting film (available from art suppliers) glued over the opening.
- A type of shadow puppetry can be performed using an overhead projector instead of a theatre. (See *Overhead projectors* and *Project-o-graph*)

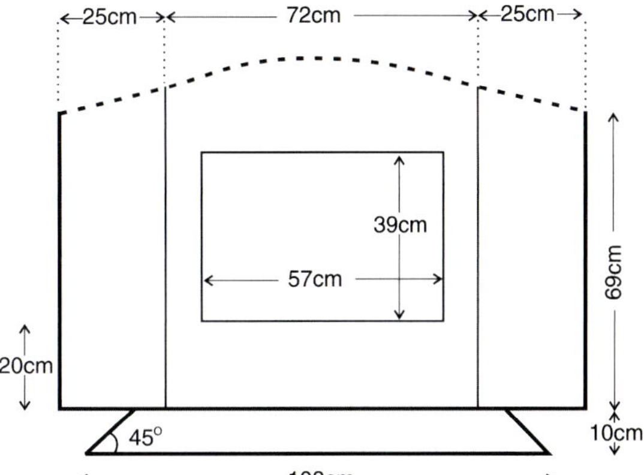

Top tips for shadow puppets

- Twist the control rod slightly clockwise and counter-clockwise to simulate walking by the slight swinging of the lower abdomen and legs.
- To reverse a puppet's direction you will need to cut a duplicate puppet which has its control rod fitted to the opposite side.
- Attach props to the puppet or add them to a duplicate puppet.
- Nod the puppet slightly to indicate conversation.

Mouth-opening puppets (MOPs)

MOPs have an unrivalled place in drawing crowds, chatting with audiences, making announcements, aiding with crowd control, awarding prizes, revising previous talks, teaching memory verses and other similar roles. Tight scripting is impractical, so the puppet needs to have a personality to guide the questions it asks, the responses it makes and the vocabulary it uses. The personality of a MOP gains credibility with its audience by how it responds to what's going on and by 'talking' about what it 'thinks', and 'feels'.

Top tips for using MOPs

- The puppet voice is part of its character. If you and your puppet are both visible to the audience, practise distracting the audience's attention so they don't notice your lips moving when your puppet speaks. Do this by deliberately looking in the appropriate directions when conversing and by giving the puppet useful things to hold, examine, give out, and so on.

- Practise 'lip synch' in front of the mirror by keeping the puppet's mouth shut when not speaking, opening the mouth for the first syllable of speech, almost closing it between every syllable and closing it on the consonants B, M and P.

- Drop the thumb (puppet's lower jaw) rather than raising the fingers (puppet's head).

- Make sure your puppet voice is not so distorted that the audience struggles to understand. Use a critical friend to report to you on its clarity and speed.

- Avoid using MOPs for dramatised Bible stories. The exception is modernised versions of parables.

- Don't have your MOPs undergoing 'spiritual experiences', praying or reading the Bible with spiritual benefit because it may convey the message that God intends salvation for stuffed toys, not boys and girls. Only living Christians and actors or puppets representing historical figures can give such personal witnesses.

quick sketching

See also ***Illustrating a story***

Quick sketching is when you sketch a picture for the audience as you tell a story. It works because audiences are naturally curious.

While they are quietly asking themselves, 'What will it be?' you have their attention long enough to speak about issues that matter.

Equipment

You'll need

- **a sturdy easel**. Plans for this are on pages 44-45.
- **a backing board**. The dimensions will depend on the size of your audience. medium density fibre (MDF) 9 mm thick, cut to 100 cm by 85 cm is usually adequate.
- **lots of paper** (trimmed to the size of the backing board) on which to practise. Make sure the paper you select works with the chalk. Butcher's paper or an end roll of newsprint is ideal.
- **hairspray** to 'fix' anything that is pre-drawn so it won't smudge. It's easy to draw over 'fixed' drawings.
- **five or more big bulldog clips** to attach paper to the backing board.
- **chalk**, preferably demonstration chalk which is big, bright and effortlessly glides over paper. It is soft, enabling each individual stick to be broken into smaller pieces. (Don't use demonstration chalk on a classroom chalkboard. It doesn't wipe off easily.) Mungyo® soft pastel, available from artist supply shops, is also good. There is a full range of colours for details and small sketches.
- **a drop sheet** to catch the chalk dust (it sticks to vinyl flooring and is difficult to remove from carpet).
- **damp rags** or wet wipes for clean up.
- **a container** with compartments to keep your chalks separated.

Decide and Dodge

Decide what you can sketch and dodge what you can't. If you need to include something from the passage – an action for instance that you can't sketch – then sketch it out of sight, or off the page, or so far in the distance that it doesn't matter.

Read through the Bible passage taking note of everything you can sketch easily. As you grow in confidence, so will your repertoire. There will most likely be

- a person (who has an occupation)
- a context (a room, a boat, a building, a piece of countryside)
- an object or animal

People

A skin-coloured ball for the head.

With black, add eyes, ears, hair and any facial features.

Eyes are two circles that touch. For females add a few little strokes for eye lashes.

blind

If you find it difficult to draw people side on, keep the person looking straight ahead and move the pupils in the eyes right or left.

A coloured box for the body. With black, add legs, arms, fabric patterns, sashes, belts and implements.

Here's a stylised representation of **Jesus**. The clothing is blue and the hair and beard is dark brown. Only the eyes, nose and mouth are black.

Buildings

Middle Eastern buildings are easy to draw. A series of boxes is all you need.

Animals

Animals can be based on a bucket and a box or a few rugby balls.

Ways of dodging

Out of sight –
There's a cow in the stable.

Off the edge of the page –
The Good Samaritan's donkey carried the injured man.

In the distance –
The shepherd began to count his sheep.

Lightning lettering

This style is based on boxes and dashes. ('I' is a thin box.) It is best used just for making a main point or identifying a character. It will lose its impact if overused.

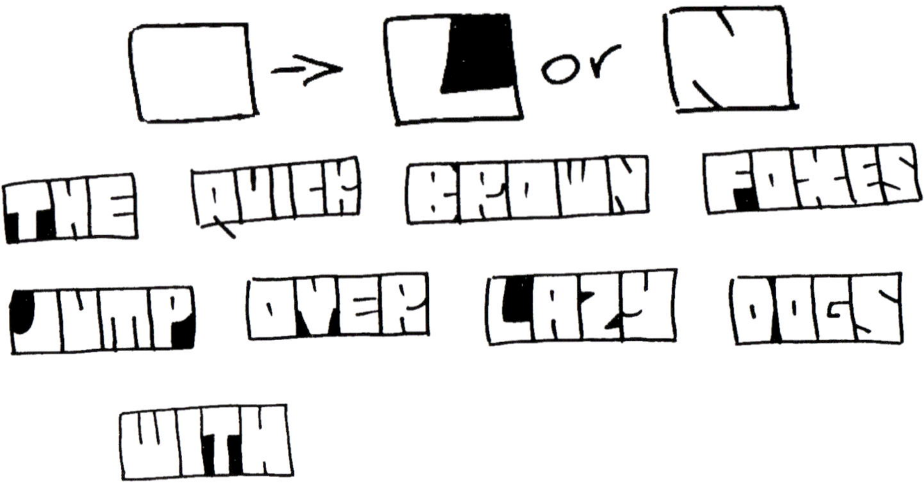

Put down a colour, then write over it with black.

Shapes

quiz games

See also ***Revision***

Quizzes are valuable for recall and revision.

Prepare your questions and answers beforehand. (It's surprising how easily your mind can go blank when making up questions on the spot.) If the participants know one another well, team contests can be fun. In this case, one group can make up the questions to challenge the other. This does not work as well when the children are strangers to each other. See *Revision* for different types of questions.

Tried and tested quiz ideas

Any of the following can be drawn up on a chart or board. Alternatively, making an attractive permanent OHP transparency means you can play the game often with little preparation. Generally, limit a game to ten minutes, even if it hasn't reached a conclusion. Better to finish while they are still keen than to allow it drag out and have some lose interest.

On rare occasions, the players may finish quickly. That's life! Immediately move on to the next part of your programme.

Noughts and Crosses

Draw up a Noughts and Crosses grid on your board or prepare an OHP transparency. Select two teams to compete with each other. Ask the teams questions in turn and, whenever a team gives a correct answer, its captain chooses a square to mark. Three noughts or three crosses in a line wins.

Vary the game by marking each square on the grid with a word.

who	where	when
why	how	what
when	where	who

In this instance, one captain at a time chooses a word. The leader asks a question of the type indicated by the word. A correct answer is rewarded by the captain marking that square with the team's symbol.

A further variation with an OHP is to prepare a transparency with pictures about the story from a previous lesson in each square of the grid. When a captain selects a picture, the question that is asked focuses on that part of the story.

Snakes and Ladders

Prepare an OHP transparency of a Snakes and Ladders chart. Prepare a box containing six ping-pong balls numbered 1 to 6. The team captains use a cardboard marker (square/triangle) to move along the rows on the transparency by the number of places shown on the ball they select. If the marker lands on the foot of a ladder, the team is asked a question. If the answer is correct, the marker moves up the ladder.

A question is also asked if the marker lands on the head of a snake. If a wrong answer is given, the marker slides down the snake. Only one answer can be offered by a team.

Run, Rabbit, Run

Use the opposite page as the basis of your gameboard.

The markers are moved by selecting a numbered ball. If the marker lands on a rabbit, a question is asked. For a correct answer, the marker moves forward the number of places shown. If the marker lands on a square with a burrow, the rabbit pops down the burrow and comes up the next burrow along the line. If the marker lands on a blackberry bush, the team misses a turn. If the marker lands on a fox, the rabbit is gobbled up and that player returns to the start.

Other board games

Make up your own board games and play with rules similar to Snakes and Ladders, with a question being asked every time a team lands on a certain symbol. Include instructions like 'miss a turn', 'swap places with the other team' and 'wait until passed'. Link with the theme of your programme or one of current interest.

Matching pairs

This works well with a new group. Prepare an acetate transparency containing twelve small pictures which match in pairs. For example, two may relate to the Christmas story, two to stories that Jesus told, two to miracles he performed. Prepare a cover page with twelve lift-up flaps with the numbers 1 to 12 pricked into them so they can be seen on the overhead. Place it over the pictures.

Ask a child in the group to choose two numbers. Lift the appropriate flaps. If the pictures are a match, the flaps are left open. If the pictures do not match, the flaps are closed and another child has a turn in choosing the next two numbers. Explain that it is best to choose one number first, and when the picture is revealed, choose the second.

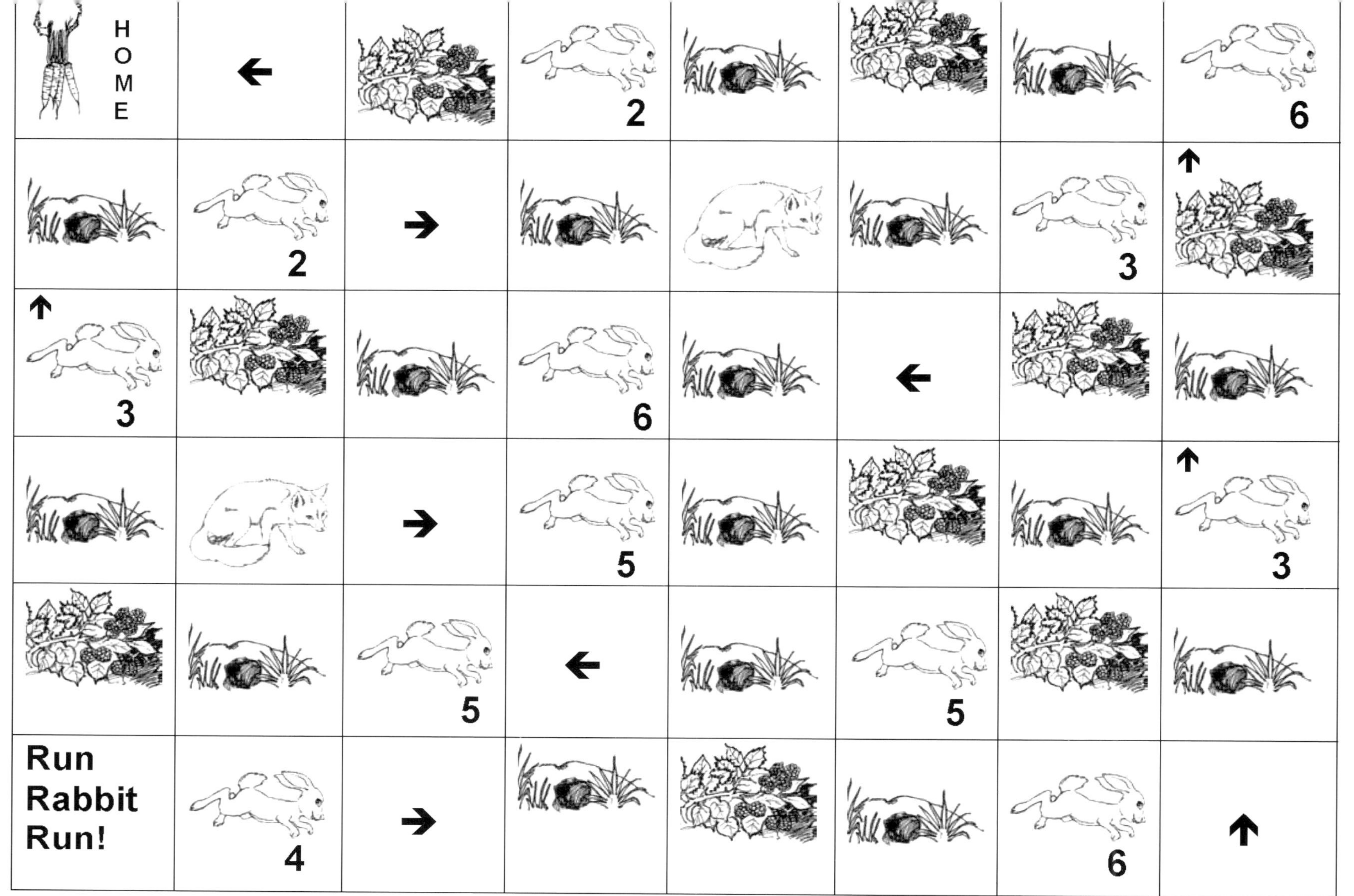
HOME
2
6
2
3
3
6
5
3
5
5
Run Rabbit Run!
4
6

relationships

See also ***Classroom management, Understanding children***

RELATIONSHIPS RELATIONSHIPS RELATIONSHI

Our relationship with children can teach them a lot about a relationship with God.

We can gain new ideas and skills to make teaching more appealing but this may have little impact if we fail in our relationships with the children. We all need to work at this. Each individual child needs to feel accepted, even those whose behaviour needs to be confronted. No doubt some children will prove to be unco-operative and difficult, but none must be written off as hopeless. Pray for the challenging children you minister amongst. There may be factors in their school or family lives which explain their attitudes, at least partially. Give time to them. Show them that you care.

What do you do if those in your group would rather not be there and are not interested? The only option is to go all out to establish a friendship with them individually. Find out if any are involved in sporting teams, and then make time to watch them play and cheer them on. Ask them about their hobbies and other interests to find some common links. Showing interest in them as individuals can help to break down their antagonism.

Developing and maintaining relationships takes time. Some in ministry think that the time is better spent teaching Bible content. The fact is, we need to do both but there's no doubt that learning is best accomplished in an environment where someone is reflecting God's love and grace. Children and young people respond positively to warmth and friendship. It's a key reason that some remain connected to the church while others don't.

In recent years, another aspect of the relationship between adults and children has become prominent. The failures of many churches to ensure only appropriate relationships between their clergy and children has been well publicised. No group can claim to be completely without problems, so we must be on the alert, not only to potential issues in the teams we lead, but also in respect to our own ministries.

The apostle Paul was able to say *You are witnesses, and so is God, of how holy, righteous and blameless we were among you* (1 Thessalonians 2:10). May each of us be able to make a similar claim.

Your church or organisation will have a safety and care policy. Scripture Union's comprehensive package *Lighting a Path to Safety* covers training and practice in child protection issues. See www.scriptureunion.org.au.

researching Bible stories

What gives a Bible talk impact? What is it that captures the audience? Enthusiasm? Participation? Relevance? Visuals? All of these deserve a place on a list of ten, but people of all ages respond to something that is important, exciting, illuminating – something they can chew over. That 'something' is gained by thoroughly researching the Bible story.

> A holiday club team member was given the task of speaking on the story of Absalom's rebellion. When he began to speak, it soon became obvious that he had not checked the story and was relying on his memory. He became hopelessly muddled by putting Joab, who was the general in charge of David's forces, on the wrong side. Those familiar with this incident in 2 Samuel 18, will appreciate something of the confusion that this created. To make matters worse, he didn't know where he had gone wrong and he floundered on, recounting a story that became more and more fictitious with every sentence. Reading that part of the Bible and others associated with it until he thoroughly understood the story would have saved him the embarrassment and the children the confusion.

What do you do when people are already very familiar with the story you've been asked to present? 'We've heard this one before!' is the chorus. This is especially so at Easter and Christmas. The great truths of the gospel story seem to lose their power because children become bored through familiarity. Many Sunday group leaders say that they have considerable difficulty teaching children because they 'already know it all'. The fact is they don't. For children familiar with the plot, digging more deeply into the Bible story will always reveal information that is new to them.

The guidelines over the page will help you to dig effectively.

Try this activity at a team training meeting sometime. Form two groups of leaders. Ask those in Group A to record as much of the story as they can from memory and ask Group B to make a list using Bibles. Generally the list that Group B compiles is more complete and more accurate than that compiled by those who are relying on their memories. Yet even Group B frequently overlooks some of the details in front of them.

Take careful note of all of the details

Many of us skim across the surface of Bible stories and ignore much of the finer detail.

Mark's account of the Lord Jesus calming the storm is the most detailed (Mark 4:35-41). Let's see how much detail there is in this incident for a leader or speaker to exploit.

- The journey began in the evening, v 35.
- The Lord had been using the boat to preach from and was already in it, v 36.
- A number of other boats accompanied them, v 36.
- Jesus fell asleep on a cushion in the stern of the boat, v 38.
- A furious storm arose, v 37.
- The waves broke over the boat, v 37.
- They were in danger of being swamped, v 37.
- The disciples woke Jesus up roughly, v 38.
- *Don't you care if we drown?* they said, v 38.
- Jesus stood up, v 39.
- He rebuked the storm with the words *Quiet, be still.* v 39.
- The wind died away and everything became completely calm, v 39.
- Jesus rebuked the disciples for their lack of faith, v 40.
- The disciples were terrified by this display of supernatural power, v 41.
- They asked each other *Who is this? Even the wind and the waves obey him!* v 41.

What facts from this summary had you previously overlooked? The time of the day the journey began? The presence of other boats? The cushion? The disciples' terror at the display of Jesus' power? Perhaps to give your presentation variety and add interest you could report the incident through the eyes of someone in one of the other boats.

Take note of the context in which the story is reported

What did Jesus teach from the incident involving the crowd of more than five thousand people recorded in John 6? When asked, most teachers explain that the Lord can supply our needs or something along those lines. But this does not answer the question. The question can only be answered by studying what comes after the feeding. John reports in verse 26 that Jesus rebuked the crowd for following *not because you saw miraculous signs but because you ate the loaves and had your fill.* He warned them of the futility of spending their energies for things that don't last. He made sure they knew that he himself is 'the bread of life' that satisfies their eternal needs. John's version adds significantly to our understanding of the incident and the message it contains.

Trace other references to the story

For new light on Old Testament stories, seek out New Testament references to them.

> A visiting speaker was invited to continue a series by addressing a school meeting about the Exodus 2 passage on Moses killing the Egyptian slave driver and fleeing. The chaplain told him, 'You can tell them that Moses was impetuous and acted on his feelings instead of waiting for God's leading. As a result he had to be disciplined by spending forty years in the desert where God moulded his character and turned him into leadership material.'

No doubt others have followed the chaplain's thinking when speaking about this passage, yet if you examine the text you'll find not even a hint of this. Moses may have been a better leader as a result of his desert experience, but it was the rejection of his leadership by the Israelites that was the reason for their additional forty years of slavery in Egypt. This is not obvious if we read Exodus 2 in isolation, but it leaps at us from the page when we turn to Stephen's speech in Acts 7. Such references need to be carefully sought out and considered.

Further light may be thrown on some incidents, particularly Old Testament stories, by seeking out reference to them in later chapters or books. For example, in Genesis 37 we read of Joseph's brothers attacking him, stripping him of his robe and throwing him into a pit. There is no indication of Joseph' s reaction to this treatment. Did he protest? Did he fight? Did he plead with them? Yes he did, but we must turn to Genesis 42:21 to discover this fact. There the brothers say to one another: *Surely we are being punished because of our brother. We saw how distressed he was when he pleaded with us for his life, but we would not listen.*

In the gospels, the raising of Lazarus (John 11:1-44) is related at length, but it's important to notice that the story doesn't stop there. In the next chapter, it is recorded that the Lord paid another visit to his friends in Bethany, and that Lazarus was one of those who shared the meal with him. He was an annoyance to the Jewish leadership, walking proof of the power of Jesus. Isn't it tragic that the chief priests immediately plotted the death of Lazarus, so recently raised from death (John 12:10)? We're not finished with the Lazarus incident even then, because a further reference is made in the account of the triumphal entry (John 12:17). The raising of Lazarus had a profound effect on the people who witnessed it. They were able to answer those who were puzzled by the Lord's arrival (Matthew 21:10). In fact it was their reports that had brought many of the people onto the streets to join the jubilant welcome in the first place (John 12:18).

Bible research often yields fascinating facts that will surprise and delight first the researcher and then their listeners.

See also ***Quiz Games***

Information encountered only once is likely to be forgotten, but if it is repeatedly reviewed, it becomes easy to recall. It has been said that teachers who don't review, leave their work half done.

Revision questions fall into two broad categories:

- **Factual questions** which ask Who, What, Where and When
- **Conceptual questions** which focus on How or Why and can be used to assess understanding.

Don't just use oral questioning. Vary your revision by using activity sheets and group games and quizzes as well as activities that require recall.

In preparing activity sheets, use a variety of ways to encourage recall

- True or false questions
- Complete the Bible verse
- Multiple choice
- Matching pairs
- Sketch the object
- Mark on a map
- 'Race against the clock' to complete the sheet

For oral quizzes try these:

- **Heads and tails** (Everyone stands while you read a statement. Hands on head = correct, tail = wrong, one hand on each = not sure.
- **Stand up/sit down** according to whether a statement is correct or incorrect.
- **Team quizzes** Form teams and allow team discussion for a set time before an answer is given.

When asking questions in a group, make it your aim for every child to be actively thinking of the answer. When an answer is given, immediately ask 'Who else was going to say that?' This lets you affirm more than just the one who answered. With some questions it's helpful to ask 'Why do you think so?' so that the children know they are expected to have an opinion of their own.

school assemblies

'The Rules'

- Find out from a school official the amount of **time** allocated for the talk and stick to it.
- **Don't be distracted.** When it's your turn to start, get on with it.
- **Give clear instructions.** Never assume that the children know instinctively what is expected of them. Confusion on the part of the leader encourages restlessness. Don't attempt to give instructions until you have succeeded in gaining the attention of the whole group.
- **All of the children need to be able to see.** If you are using a sketch board, the line of vision for the children on the extremities of the front rows may be too acute and you will need to ask for the children to be moved.
- **You need to be able to see every child**. Some assemblies are held in double classrooms where a dividing partition creates one or two dead spots where children can hide. Have such children moved, but rather than being officious, explain that you wouldn't like them to be unable to see what you have to show.
- If a sketch board or a puppet theatre is being used, the children in the **front rows** may be too close and will need to be moved back.
- **Visuals and song words** must be large enough to be clearly visible to all. See *Overhead projectors*.
- **Adults should sit at the rear or on the ends of rows** so that they don't obscure vision. A centre aisle enables you to move to check any trouble spot.
- **Maintain a professional attitude** to give the school staff confidence in you. After your presentation, maintain control until you hand back to a member of staff.

Can you see everyone in your audience? Can they all see and hear you and your sketch board or screen? Children on the extremities, especially those in the front rows, may need to move. In double classrooms and auditoriums 'hideaways' exist in the form of panels and dividers.

script writing

See also ***Drama***

The purpose of a Bible story script is to communicate a message that moves the audience one step closer to Jesus.

The message should not just involve knowledge but engage the emotions and be life-related. A well-dramatised Bible story can help people understand how God has interacted with people in the past and help them wonder if or how God is doing that in their lives now.

The Bible was written to be read, not performed, so 'sanctified imagination' is needed to add details that increase visual and dramatic interest. These just fill in the gaps in the Bible record and must always be consistent with what is written. They must never contradict Scripture.

Guidelines for scripting drama

A good play centres on conflict
Conflict creates suspense and, through resolution of conflict, the audience experiences satisfaction. First, determine the main and any secondary conflicts, and the means of their resolutions.

Determine the sequence of the action
Strive for an original angle on a well-known story. For example, script the events of Christmas through the eyes of the gatekeeper of Bethlehem. As a first step, produce a synopsis of what he might have done.

Limit the use of narration
Portray action visually or with sound effects rather than through words.

Avoid long speeches and flowery language
In the main, use colloquial language and only a sentence or two at a time.

Avoid description of people and places
The audience can use their eyes and their imagination.

Balance the acts so that they are approximately the same duration

Ensure that the time is consistent with the nature of the play
There are different types of time that need to be considered.

- **Audience time** This is the length of time the play will take to perform.
- **Story time** The period covered by the story; it ranges from minutes to years.
- **Period time** The century in which the play is set. As biblical incidents are historical, it is best that the play reflects that period rather than giving it a modern setting. Parables can be the exception.

Be aware of the physical movement of the actors
The script must allow time for the movement of the actors on and off the stage. If a character needs to change costumes between an exit and a re-entrance, the script must allow enough time.

Use humour where appropriate
While the biblical record is probably never intentionally humorous, there are some flashes that are amusing, such as Elijah taunting the prophets of Baal. Humour provides your audience with release of emotional tension, so inject it into your script where appropriate.

Depict mood honestly
Don't treat something casually that is actually urgent. Don't depict in a light-hearted fashion a scene that should be serious.

Bring out the basic conflicts early, keep the focus on them, and resolve them at the end of the play. Conflicts can be right versus wrong, man versus nature, man versus himself, man versus God, good versus a greater good.

In the case of David and Goliath, David is in conflict with Goliath. But in the case of Naaman, what was he fighting against? It's not his leprosy but his pride that's the key. Because Naaman's problem was his pride, your opening scene should focus on pride in some way. Perhaps a beggar is forced to move aside to make way for Naaman's passing. As he exits, the beggar mutters 'Mark my words, the day will come when that leper will step aside for me.'

Allow the play to communicate its own message
Avoid the temptation to include preaching in the script.

There is a difference between surprise and suspense
A detective is searching for clues. He opens a cupboard and a dead body falls out. That is surprise. If, on the other hand, the audience know that the body is in the cupboard, suspense builds each time he approaches the cupboard door.

Be cautious when inventing names for characters in biblical plays
Your audience, especially the children, may think that these were truely their names. We do not know the name of Cleopas' companion, for example, and it is best not to invent one. Parables can be the exception to this.

serial stories

When movies were still new, many children went every Saturday to 'the flicks'. One of the main attractions at the cinema in those days was the serial. The adventures of fictional heroes like The Lone Ranger, Hopalong Cassidy, Buck Rogers or Flash Gordon held audiences intrigued. Each episode ended with a cliff hanger situation and all were keen to return next week to find out what happened.

Classic stories such as *Pilgrim's Progress, The Lion, the Witch and the Wardrobe* and others of the Narnia stories work well in serial form. Patricia St John's *Treasures of the Snow* is also a good story to serialise.

A delightful contemporary book that can be read a chapter at a time to a group of 5 to 10-year-olds is *Shivery* by Faith Duffy. The story is about a shepherd and his sheep and it gives hope to children facing tough issues.

Scripture Union publishes these holiday club programmes which contain serial drama scripts: *Knock Knock, On-Line: Connecting and communicating with God* and *Wet, Wild and Wonderful*. Others which have an accompanying DVD or video are *Xpedition Force, Desert Detectives, MEGAQUEST, Seaside Rock, Groundbreakers* and more. Check out www.scriptureunion.org.au, www.scriptureunion.org.uk, www.scriptureunion.org.nz

singing

Bright singing can be an attractive feature of a children's or family programme.

It helps to instil a sense of community and there's no doubt that setting words to music helps us to remember them. But don't fall into the trap of letting singing take up practically all of your opening session just because the children appear to be enjoying it. Many children enjoy singing, but some find more than a little singing tedious.

The TRIM test, taken from Scripture Union's music collection *Gospelling to the Beat*, is a good guide for selecting songs.

T	Does the song teach what is True and worthy?
R	Are the words Related to life?
I	Is the song Interesting? Are the words memorable?
M	Do the words Make sense to children?

Popular musical styles change constantly, but these guidelines remain valid.

Top tips for singing

- **Select the songs in advance**
  There's a place for the 'Who has a favourite' approach but choose most of the songs for the session in advance and make sure you have the music required.

- **Know the words and tune well**
  To lead a song with confidence and enthusiasm you need to know it well so you can keep eye contact.

- **Remember that 'familiarity breeds contempt'**
  In a holiday club, teach a new song every day. In a more regular activity such as a weekly after-school club, set the target of learning a new song once a month.

- **Avoid duplication**
  Have some music that is the hallmark of your club rather than using only the songs that the children sing elsewhere.

- **Use a variety of styles**
  Noisy rollicking songs are fun but include some quieter and more melodious ones as well.

- **Choose music for effect**
  Music can be a powerful conveyer of mood. When a group sings raucous songs they are likely to become upbeat and difficult to manage. Choose a gentle song to settle them down before the next activity.

- **Briefly explain unfamiliar words and concepts**

- **Don't try to lead the singing and operate equipment at the same time**
  If you plan to use CDs for backing music, you'll need a technical assistant who can take their eye off the children to find the right track.

It's probably true that the songs we teach will be remembered long after the things we say have faded. Choose wisely.

> A mission leader revisiting a holiday club after ten years was approached by a young man resplendent in bikie leathers. 'Hi! Remember me?' The leader's mind went back to a mischievous boy who delighted in displaying his skill at climbing the centre pole of the marquee.
>
> 'Sure Ricky. How could I possibly forget you!'
>
> They chatted for a few moments and then Ricky asked, 'Do you still sing *Wide, Wide as the Ocean?*'
>
> 'We sure do! God's love is still as great as ever.'
>
> Despite the lapse of ten years, the words of that chorus were still fresh in his memory.

See also ***Aims, Dialogue, Enthusiasm, Links in storytelling, Zest***

Visualise the scene

To produce movies like *The Passion of the Christ*, film directors need to be able to visualise the events reported in the biblical records, and then direct the participating actors to recreate those visualisations for the camera. In a similar way, storytellers need to have already visualised the incidents they are describing.

Consider, for example, the report of the cleansing of the temple as reported in John 2:14-16. From the record it's clear that the reason for the Lord's drastic action was that the traders had turned his *Father's house into a market.* Let the scene impact all your senses.

Can you hear the shouts of the traders canvassing their wares? Can you hear the murmurs of the worshippers bartering for the livestock they wished to purchase? Can your mind recreate the lowing of the cattle, the bleating of the sheep, the cooing of the doves and the clinking of the coins? All of these would have made quiet contemplation by the temple worshippers very difficult.

Add to that the stench of the yarded animals, and is it any wonder that Jesus reacted as he did? Can you visualise the confusion that must have followed as Jesus raged through the market, opening the pens, overturning the money tables, cracking his whip and shouting at the dove sellers to 'Get these out of here!' Can you see in your mind's eye the moneychangers clawing desperately among the heaps of cow dung for their precious coins while the terrified animals milled to and fro in confused mobs?

'Hear' the voices

Not only do we need to visualise the scene, we need to 'hear the voices'.

As the hubbub of that riotous scene began to abate, the Jewish leaders challenged Jesus' actions. Can you hear the indignation in their voices as they protest 'What miraculous sign can you show us to prove your authority to do all this?'

Jesus' reply, 'Destroy this temple, and I will raise it again in three days', had them bewildered.

'It has taken forty-six years to build this temple and you are going to raise it in three days?' One can imagine them adding 'That's ridiculous!'

Identifying the emotion with which their words were expressed and recreating this as you recount the event is one of the main tools of storytelling.

Convey the emotions

To bring alive for your hearers the emotions felt by the characters, we have to first develop a feel for those characters from the text.

Some preachers tend to focus on the academic aspects of the Bible accounts and overlook the dramatic and emotional. They research their subject faithfully and give us the benefit of their research by informing us that the force of a word in the original language has a certain meaning.

> In a sermon on Nehemiah, the preacher drew attention to the fact that there was a space of about four months between the time Nehemiah heard of the depressing state of Jerusalem and his confrontation with King Artaxerxes.

That fact adds to our understanding of the event but what significance does it have to our appreciation of the account?

It is highly significant in fact. Nehemiah records that when he heard of Jerusalem's depressing state he *sat down and wept* because he was deeply moved. For some days he *mourned and fasted and prayed.* Despite his inner distress, he managed to put on a brave face whenever he approached the king until the day of his request.

In telling this story how would you dramatise it? When the king asked *Why does your face look so sad when you are not ill? This can be nothing but sadness of heart* we have to remember that these are the words of a despot who was suspicious that Nehemiah may be part of a plot against him. There must have been a strong tone of suspicion in the way he spoke, because his words struck terror in Nehemiah's heart (Nehemiah 2:2). It is essential that children's speakers take note of such emotional aspects of a passage and convey them by using dramatic speech at every opportunity.

King Belshazzar's feast in Daniel 5 is one of the most dramatic moments in the whole of the Scriptures. While the nobles of Babylon were feasting, the fingers of a human hand appeared and wrote on the plaster of the wall. When he saw it, the king's mouth dropped open (suit your expression to the statement when you're relating this). He stared in amazement as the letters of the mysterious message appeared.

'Wha…wha...wha...what's happening?' he stammered. 'Wha...wha...what does this mean? Quickly!' he shrieked. 'Call the enchanters and the astrologers! Find someone who can explain this...this...eh...m...me...message!'

The passage tells us that *the king's face turned pale and he was so frightened that his knees knocked together and his legs gave way.* You can convey the king's terror by using stammering speech and pointing with a trembling hand. It's a little more difficult to make your knees knock, but you can try!

The story of the search for a wife for Isaac (Genesis 24) can be used for a talk about prayer. There's little action of note in the story but a study of the emotions mentioned is very revealing.

The servant's emotions

From the outset the servant was apprehensive, asking Abraham *What if the woman is unwilling to come back with me?* (Gen 24:5) Verse 12 records his prayer and in verse 15 we read that *before he had finished praying Rebekah came out with her jar on her shoulder.* No wonder he was so astonished when, on requesting a drink from Rebekah, she offered to draw water for his camels as well. After a long journey, a camel can drink nearly 100 litres of water. There were ten camels, so Rebekah hauled a tonne of water to the surface, running it in a pottery jar to the camels' trough. No wonder verse 21 says that without saying a word, *the man watched her closely*, overcome with astonishment that his prayer had been answered so promptly. When he asked her family connections, Rebekah had all the right credentials. He was so overcome that he fell flat on his face and praised God.

At Rebekah's home her family offered lavish hospitality, but the servant was so full of the astonishing sequence of the events that he refused to eat until he related what had happened. In response to his story, the family agreed that Rebekah could become Isaac's bride. This brought a further emotional outburst of gratitude from the servant as once again *he bowed down to the ground before the Lord* (verse 52).

In verse 54 we see him relaxed, eating, drinking and settling down for the night. Next morning he is eager to return home but his hosts are reluctant for Rebekah to leave so soon. His apprehension wells up again as he protests at being detained. It must have given him considerable satisfaction when, on his arrival home, he *told Isaac all he had done* (verse 66).

Rebekah's emotions

We must remember too that while Rebekah's reactions aren't as easy to identify, she was not a passive participant in this drama. When Abraham's servant asked her for a drink, her response was instantaneous as she *quickly lowered her jar* (verse 17). There is a hint of excitement in her movements as she emptied her jar into the trough and *ran* back to the well to draw more water. What thoughts went through her mind as the man gave her a gold nose ring and two gold bracelets? She must have had some realisation of what was afoot. This type of thing didn't happen every day! Her words expressed eagerness as she informed him that he would be welcome at their home (verse 25). Her excitement was obvious when *she ran and told her mother's household about these things* (verse 28).

Bring the narrative to life through actions

Never just state a fact if you can 'bring it to life'

The Bible records that when David went to meet Goliath, he was armed only with his sling and *five smooth stones.* You could baldly state this fact to your audience or you could bring it to life by pretending to be David as he carefully selected those stones – picking up a stone and discarding it because it was either too flat or too rough or too light, then placing another in an imaginary pouch because it had the smooth surface he was looking for.

When you do this, you are enacting this part of the story very much the way it must have happened. It is legitimate to fill in some details in the Bible story using your 'sanctified imagination' so long as what you say falls into the category of probability.

Use sound effects

It is difficult to explain the use of sound effects in writing, and we can end up with the equivalent of a Batman comic with its 'wham', 'bam', 'zap' and 'bop' captions. Despite this limitation, it's worth mentioning that good children's speakers use descriptive sound effects.

David's stone went 'clunk' against Goliath's forehead, the giant staggered back and went 'neeeeowww vump' on the ground.

The purpose of these sound effects is to help your story live. Be careful not to overdo them. Any sound effect, expression or gesture that draws attention to itself will detract from, rather than enhance, the effectiveness of your talk.

Internalise the text

The Network of Biblical Storytellers (NOBS) encourages the storyteller to memorise (the Network prefers 'internalise') the text of a modern Bible translation and recite it graphically with attention to tone, expression and gesture. While this could be difficult to achieve if you're storytelling often, it provides variety and is worth the work involved.

The tempo of a good meeting for children can be described as 'unhurried haste'.

Children thrive on variety, so pack into your programme as many different features as practical. Move briskly from one item to another, avoiding anything that drags. As a rough guide, each section of the overall programme should be no longer than ten minutes. The exception may be the talk which could stretch to fifteen minutes.

Each member of your team should know the programme, what comes immediately before their part and how long their segment is to take, so that the whole meeting flows smoothly. As one person leaves the platform, the next must be already arriving. Your role as overall leader is to keep everything flowing smoothly. There may even be times when it will be necessary to interrupt in order to hurry things along.

Train your team to be focused about all they do. Each person should start straight in on the segment of the programme allocated to them, and not hark back to something that has previously happened.

If you have a visitor to introduce, be brief and let them get started. If the leader takes five minutes to say how wonderful the speaker is and how privileged they are to have him come to visit them, it may be difficult for that speaker to regain the attention of the children. Don't warn them to be on their best behaviour either. This is an unconscious vote of no confidence in the visitor's ability to interest the children.

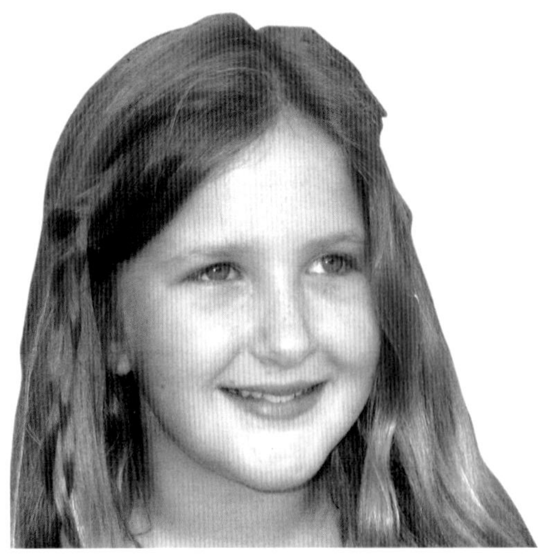

understanding children

See also ***Relationships***

Jesus called a little child and had him stand among his disciples. And he said: *I tell you the truth, unless you change and become like little children you will never enter the kingdom of heaven.*

At face value that's very simple statement, yet it's been the subject of thousands of sermons and many hours of intense discussion. What does it mean to be 'like little children'?

What are little children like? While you don't need a degree in child psychology to take on the responsibility of teaching and nurturing children, you do need some basic insights into what children are like in order to communicate with them successfully.

Observe

Watching and listening to children is the best way to understand them.

One of the founders of the Scripture Union movement, Tom Bishop, made a point of eavesdropping on groups of children. This enabled him to know what activities were of interest to children. As the movement developed, he began publishing a series of monthly magazines for different age groups. *The Boys Magazine* and *The Girls Magazine* catered for older children, while *Our Own Magazine* was for younger ones. Those early Scripture Union magazines had a huge circulation for many years. Bishop's editorial touch sprang from his keen observation of children.

As well as observing children, watch those workers who appear to be successful in capturing and maintaining the interest of children. Do not assume that they are more gifted than you are. While this may be true to some extent, the secret is that they have developed skills that you can learn. Analyse what they do and why – and learn from them for your own ministry.

Watch children's television, in particular those programmes which children talk about. This enables you to join in their conversation. Without being judgmental about what they watch, you can sometimes ask children 'Do you think that was a good thing to do?' This can help them think about some of the moral standards that underlie what they see on the screen.

Offer friendship

The best children's workers are those who are prepared to spend a lot of time with children. Many adults ignore the presence of children. Even in camps and after-school

clubs, it is common to see adult or teen leaders associating more with the other team members than with the children.

The first step towards friendship with children is being able to converse freely with them. Ask their opinions and listen carefully. Informal group activities, such as a trip to a zoo, museum or other place of interest, are good for getting to know each other better. So are craft and games.

Excellent books which provide a window into the world of children are *Children Finding Faith* by Francis Bridger, *Kids' Culture* by Nick Harding and the *Working with…* series from Scripture Union.

Remember your own childhood

Did you like pumpkin when you were very young? Keep in mind the things you liked and disliked as a child. Try to recall your feelings when you were their age. Put yourself in the children's shoes. Some leaders, who as children hated people praying long prayers, now inflict on children the very same thing.

venues

See also ***School Assemblies***

Each setting has its challenges, but there are certain guidelines that apply to them all.

Creating atmosphere

Create a welcoming atmosphere with good lighting, bright colours and decorations. Time spent tidying up can work wonders for the general atmosphere and show children that we think they are worth some effort. Music before and after the programme adds to the atmosphere.

Seating

Arrange rows of seats close together to avoid the children moving their chairs forward. If the programme is held out of doors, don't have the children looking into the sun or with the wind coming directly into their faces. If there are no chairs, a sheet of thick plastic to sit on helps bring and keep the group together. Stand in front of a wall so the children aren't distracted by what's behind you. Avoid standing in front of a window.

Sound

Check that audio equipment is working and that the sound will be adequate when the hall is full of sound-absorbing bodies. If extra amplification isn't available, place your player above head level to allow the sound to carry.

Ventilation

Fresh air will stop your audience nodding off.

Lighting

Avoid high platforms and lights behind the speaker. Spotlights on the stage make it difficult for the speaker to see the audience. Ensure that the whole audience can see and hear both the speaker and any visuals.

Props

Dispense with a stand if you can so that you can be closer to the audience. If you need a place for notes or visual aids, use a small table at your side, not a lectern between you and your audience.

Access

Don't seat children in doorways. Make sure exits are kept clear at all times.

video-making

Making a video helps focus people on an issue or story and gets them involved.

With the new advances in computer software and digital cameras, the sky's the limit for those with good technical know-how. But if that isn't you, then don't panic, you can still create a unique and captivating story with a basic video camera. A video is made using moving pictures not moving cameras. If you have a tripod this will help avoid the seasick feeling for your audience. The more you involve the children in production, the more they will own and remember the concepts addressed.

Here are some simple ideas for making a video:

- Acting and recording a well known Bible story. Talk about the setting and how to portray what happens, then do a rough script and get filming
- Plan and make a music video to a Christian song
- Record a fictional or personal story
- Video short and snappy interviews with children
- Investigate a topic in 'current affair' style

visi-wheel stories

Never seen a visi-wheel? It's simple really! It's designed to be used with an overhead projector but can be adapted for PowerPoint®.

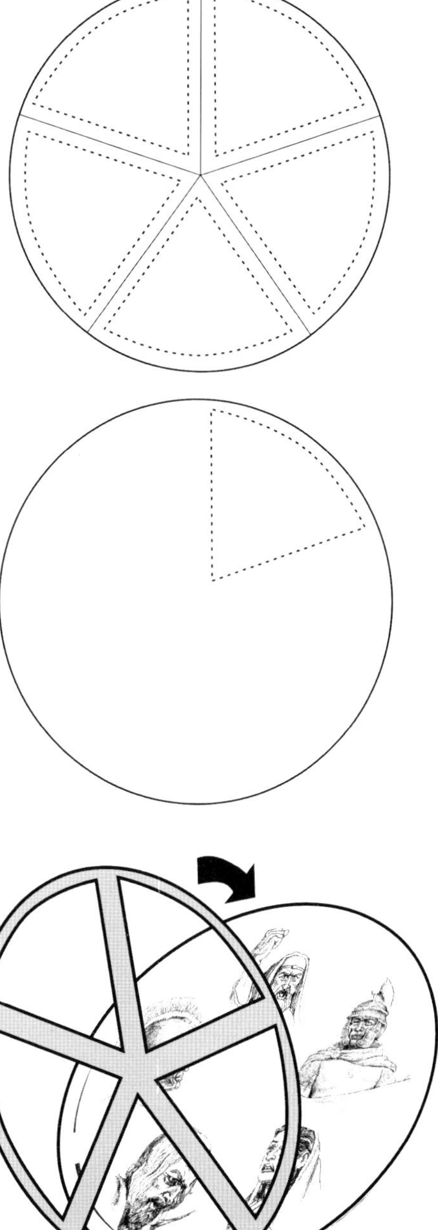

Making a visi-wheel

1. Mark out a circle about 20 cm in diameter on a piece of cardboard. Mark five sections as shown. Draw two dotted lines about 5 mm on each side of the lines which form the sections, from the centre to the edge of the circle. Cut out the sections along the dotted lines. The strips of cardboard between the segments will look like the spokes of a wheel and will provide stability. This is your base card.

2. Cut out a second circle slightly larger than the first, and cut out just one sector from it.

3. Mount the story acetate transparency on the base card, with the spokes uppermost. Take care to line up the spokes of the visi-wheel with the gaps between the pictures, so that nothing is missing when the pictures appear on the screen. Secure with masking tape.

4. Place the second wheel on top. A split pin through the axis of both cards will allow you to move the wheel over each of the pictures in turn.

Visi-wheel story – Onlookers to the crucifixion

This story focuses on the emotions of the people who were present at the crucifixion of Jesus.

Talk outline

Begin by discussing emotion and the way we reveal what we feel by the look on our faces. This is your big your opportunity to practise pulling exaggerated faces.

When we're happy, we look like this [smile]. When we're angry, we look like this [scowl]. When we're bored...

When Jesus was crucified a large crowd of people gathered on the hill outside the city to watch him die. Why were they there?

Some went to make fun of him.
Display the angry leader picture.

Describe the crowd and graphically re-enact the scene by repeating their ridicule as recorded in Luke 23:35, Mark 15:29-32 and Matthew 27:39-43. Discuss with your class why it was that these people were so antagonistic towards Jesus. John 19:7 and Matthew 27:18 tell us why. There are people like them today.

Some were there because it was their job.
Display the picture of the soldiers.

Describe the soldiers who divided up Jesus' clothes and gambled for his undergarments from John 19:23-24. These men just couldn't care less. From their point of view, the crucifixion of Jesus was nothing to do with them. They were only interested in what they could get out of it. The one who won the toss and went home with Jesus' coat must have been very pleased. I wonder how long the coat lasted before it wore out.

A few were very distressed.
Display the picture of Mary.

Recount the incident described in John 19:25-27 and Mark 15:40. As Mary stood there, she may have remembered the warning given to her by the prophet Simeon at the time of Jesus' birth described in Luke 2:35.

Some didn't want to be there at all.
Display the picture of the dying thief.

The two thieves who were crucified at the same time would rather have been anywhere but there. Describe the conversation reported in Luke 23:39-43. Point out that, to begin with, both men sneered at Jesus (Matthew 27:44).

Explain the purpose of Jesus' death, pointing out that the repentant thief was forgiven and given the promise that he would be with Jesus. We can experience forgiveness like the thief if we are willing to put our trust in him.

At least one came to realise who Jesus is.
Display the picture of the Roman soldier.

Describe a centurion's responsibilities. The centurion in charge of the squad of soldiers realised that Jesus wasn't like other criminals he'd executed. *When the centurion heard Jesus' cry and saw how he died he said, 'Surely this man was the Son of God.'* (Mark 15:39) Compare Matthew 27:50-54 and Luke 23:44-47.

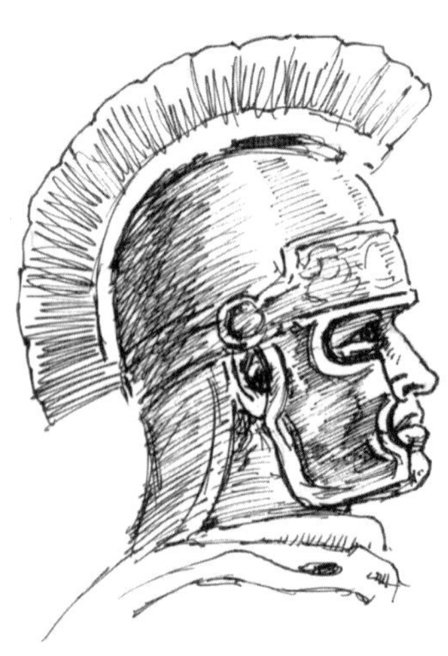

Now you know how these people reacted. You live many centuries after this happened, but how do you feel about Jesus dying?

See also ***Advertising, Flashcard pictures, Illustrating a story, Publicity, Quick sketching, Writing***

We are competing for attention in a visual age. To *attract and hold attention* we need to include visuals. They help arouse curiosity, generating opportunities to communicate.

The biblical era seems light years away from our time. Visuals can **assist understanding**. If the children we teach have never seen a sheep, then lessons about lost sheep may miss the mark with them.

Imagine trying to describe a banana to people who had never seen one. 'Well er it's a fruit. It's yellow with a black tip at each end. It's shaped like a half-moon or um ah a sort of a hook.' What would help more is if you passed around some bananas so that your class could see them, touch them, smell them and taste them.

Descriptions of life in Bible times can be difficult to grasp and terribly boring. An object, a model or a picture can quickly overcome the problem. Visuals also help to make your message memorable.

> In a session about Nehemiah, the leader started with 'this is just what it looked like' as he emptied a heap of hearth bricks onto a table.
>
> All eyes were on the bricks (which happened to have cards with the main points of his talk attached to one side). He continued, 'In Nehemiah's day, that's how the city of Jerusalem was described. A heap of bricks! When Nehemiah heard about it, he was very sad.'
>
> The leader produced the first of the labelled bricks and recounted that part of the story, repeating this with each new point, finally transforming the untidy heap into a neat wall. The initial interest didn't wane at all as the story unfolded.

Top tips for producing visual aids

- **Make them large** – Visuals should be large enough to be easily seen by all.
- **Use colour carefully** – Lettering should be in strong colours.
- **Use lower case letters, not capitals, on charts.**
- **Be neat.**
- **Keep it simple** – Many have known the embarrassment of having too many cards or pieces of equipment that somehow got muddled up as the talk progressed.
- **Don't let them distract from the message.**
- **Keep them uncluttered without too much detail.**
- **Be age appropriate** – There is little point in using word charts for children who can't read. Older children won't be impressed with childish pictures.
- **Be culturally appropriate** – Visuals must be contemporary and so must the means of showing them.
- **Be original and imaginative** – Homemade visuals can very effective, but making them can take considerable time. Consider involving some of the skilled teenagers or retirees from your church to help you produce your own visuals.
- **Variety rules!** – Use as many different visual tools as you can comfortably manage in a session.

voice

Your voice is a key instrument to convey your message so you will do well to give some attention to its development. It's not the voice, but the way you take control of it and use it that makes it such an asset. Each of us should work at clear diction and clarity of expression.

Top tips for using your voice well

- **Open your mouth.** Don't mumble.
- **Practise often.** There will be less hesitancy in your presentation; fewer 'ums', 'ahs' and 'ers'. Accept every opportunity to speak in public.
- **Work on your voice with determination.** Sing (even if only in the shower). Whistle (it flexes the lips). Read aloud. Practise deep breathing. The voice is built up by exercise just as the biceps are.
- **Practise projecting your voice.** Volume and force are not the same thing as shouting. Volume demands the open throat and full clear tones.
- **Record and critically listen to yourself.** Some of us end sentences with 'OK' or 'right'. Some pop a 'yeah' in the middle of a sentence. Look for bad habits in your speech and work on eliminating them.

wonder wall

WONDER WALL WONDER WALL WONDER WALL WONDER W

A wonder wall is a fabric-covered board for displaying visual aids.

Making a wonder wall

Use medium density fibre board (MDF), 120 cm by 90 cm for large audiences perhaps half that size for a classroom.

Choose a non-shiny fabric that accepts hook-and-loop tape like Velcro®.
Ask for 'noticeboard fabric'. Test it before you buy. A dark colour, like black or dark blue is ideal. Avoid orange and red.

Completely PVA-glue the fabric to the board, not just around the edges. For a professional look, include a frame around the edge.

What to put on it

Here are just some of many things that can be displayed on a wonder wall.

- Words printed on coloured cardboard.
  These could be key words from a lesson or talk, or text for a memory verse.
  A manageable supply of card is coloured manilla folders.
- Your own illustrations, artwork or enlarged clip art illustrations.
- Flannelgraph figures.
- Cardboard graphics that you make yourself like symbols and arrows.
- Quiz games, like noughts and crosses.
- Black silhouettes of figures placed onto yellow fabric.
  (Choose illustrations of people that face sideways.)

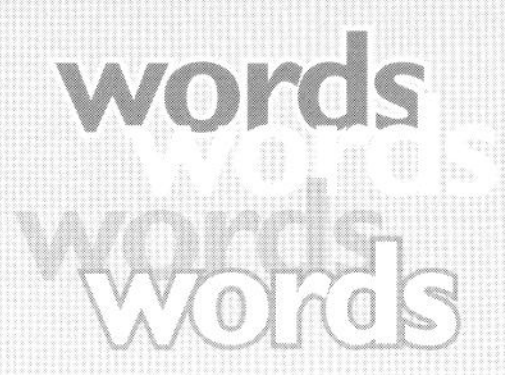

words

See also ***Dialogue***

Words are the building blocks of storytelling, and your choice of words matters in involving and delighting your hearers. Words should not attract attention to themselves, but to the ideas that they express.

When relating Bible stories, get into the habit of using colourful words. Vivid, evocative and unusual words help them to picture mentally the events described. For example, rather than 'said', these words are more colourful...

> mumbled, muttered, stammered, stuttered, grumbled, grizzled, whinged, whispered, shouted, chattered

How much more appealing are 'gobbled' and 'gulped' than 'ate'? Instead of merely walking, a character could

> stride, rush, amble, trudge, march, tiptoe, stagger or slink.

Consider the words in these Bible stories

- When telling how David and Abishai crept into King Saul's camp, saying they 'slithered' evokes the mental image of a snake-like movement.
- In the meeting between Jesus and Zacchaeus, the New International Version in Luke 19:7 reports that all of the people began to 'mutter'.
- Sometimes you can create an exciting effect by stringing together a set of descriptive adjectives. For example: King Nebuchadnezzar made a great big, enormous, tremendous, stupendous, fantastic, magnificent image!
- Use alliteration like 'down in the deepest, darkest, dingiest, dirtiest, dampest dungeon in Jerusalem was a man in chains – Barabbas'.

Become alert to the words used in good children's literature. Learn from expert writers, but be a critical observer and develop a personal style of your own that feels comfortable.

Suit your language to your audience, avoiding terms and phrases that are beyond the understanding of children. It is especially important to use the colloquial language of everyday conversation. These days, for example, Australians would never say 'He scorned it', but rather 'He rubbished it'. The latter borders on slang but, more importantly, it is a phrase that children would be familiar with and relate to. Most authors writing on public speaking, oppose the use of slang but it can be helpful, providing you use expressions common in everyday speech. Only use slang that is part of your normal speech, not to impress your audience. Children won't understand what you are trying to do and teenagers will despise your efforts to ingratiate yourself.

Diction and pronunciation have an important part to play in verbal communication so it's wise to include in your personal library some books on public speaking, and speech in general.

writing

See also ***Bubble writing, Quick sketching***

When writing for children, both for display purposes and for handouts, use simple familiar letters.

Young children will not be able to read 'running writing', so try to use the script that is used in their school and practise until you can do it well. And for writing on a board, practice with large letters on a vertical surface at home. It is so different from writing at a desk!

Books of instruction for school scripts are available at local newsagents or book stores or, if you minister in school, ask the classroom teacher.

Top tips for the blackboard or whiteboard

- Use a script that's familiar to the children.
- Make the letters large enough for everyone to read easily.
  (Don't guess. Go to the back of the room and see if you can read it.)
- Use upper and lower case letters. Don't write all in capitals, except for bubble writing or lightning lettering.
- Use colour where possible to add interest.
- Write new or unfamiliar words on the board so that the children can see the correct spelling. They will also remember them better.

zest

The zest that we bring to our programmes springs largely from our attitude.

Whether presenting a message, running a game, demonstrating craft, producing a leaflet, conducting a quiz, leading singing or organising a programme, if it's done enthusiastically, the children will respond positively.

The apostle Paul expressed it this way

> *Whatever you do, work at it with all your heart, as working for the Lord, not for men...It is the Lord Christ you are serving (Colossians 3:23-24).*

Code of practice for those who work with children

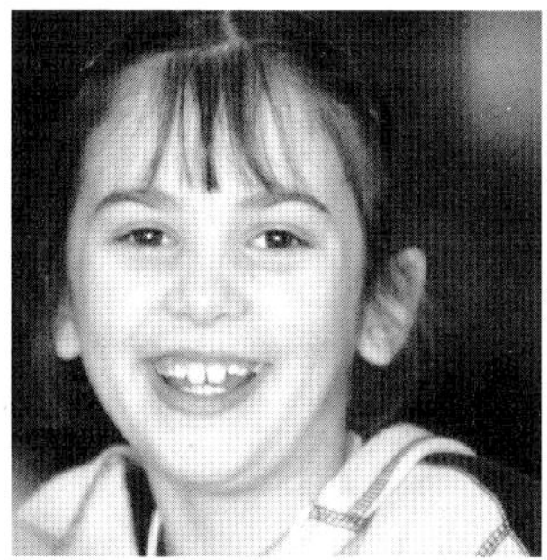

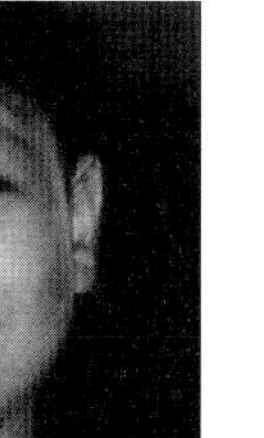

We will seek to reflect God's care for all children, at all times.

We will be up-to-date and well informed about the requirements of the duty of care legislation laid down by governments. This will include additional requirements made by our organisation or for a particular activity.

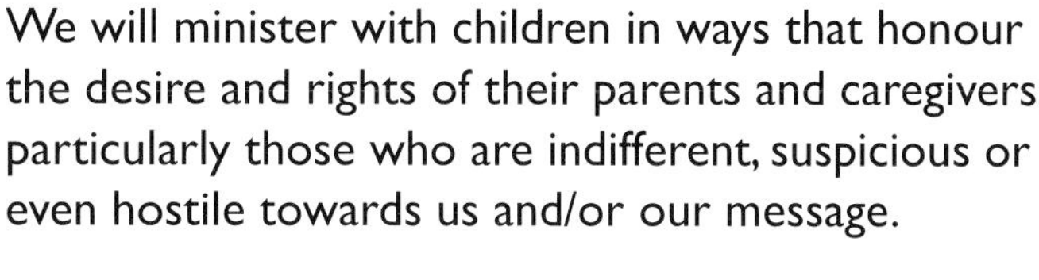

We will minister with children in ways that honour the desire and rights of their parents and caregivers, particularly those who are indifferent, suspicious or even hostile towards us and/or our message.

We will work to ensure the emotional safety of every child. We want every child to feel valued and included and their opinions respected.

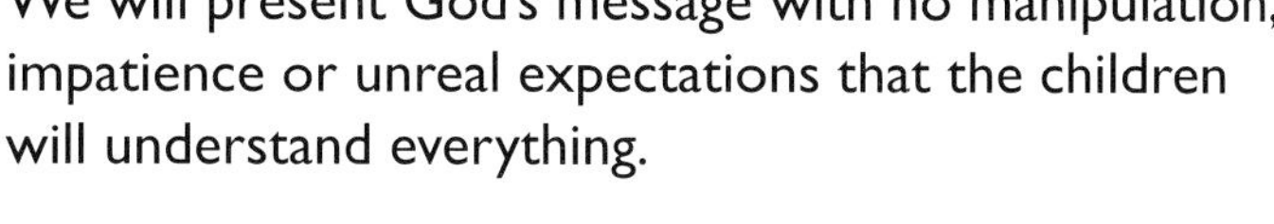

We will present God's message with no manipulation, impatience or unreal expectations that the children will understand everything.

We will be sensitive towards children from other cultures. We will use words that are easy for them to understand and we will respect their backgrounds.

We will remember that children have different temperaments, strengths and rates of development. We will value individual differences.

We will seek to introduce children to Jesus, the Bible and the Church because the best thing a boy or girl can do is to know God and live as God's child.

children's ministry
Is it worth the effort?

For a number of years I was involved in a bi-annual children's worker training seminar at Tahlee Bible College in partnership with Ron Schravemade, a missioner with the Newcastle-based Gospel Service Mission. In the opening session of one seminar, Ron's address was entitled *Any mug can do it!* His objective was to persuade the participants that such things as quick sketching, puppetry and drama were within the scope of their abilities. My session that followed was *Only the best will do!* My purpose was to demonstrate that there is always room for improvement in whatever we do. Children's ministry takes in these two extremes.

As each new batch of teachers, kids' club leaders, camp staff or beach mission team members start in ministry, most of what they learn comes through observing others. Some of what they see will be excellent and some will not. Whether you've been in ministry for many years or are just getting started, do not be content with the mediocre, but strive for excellence.

Since retiring from the full-time staff of Scripture Union in New South Wales, I've seized numerous opportunities to speak at school assemblies, in company with Albert Able of Outback Ministries. Audiences have sometimes consisted of hundreds of children in packed halls or playgrounds. At other times there are only six or seven pupils in outback communities. In each instance, we have struggled into the school with a board and easel, a screen and OHP and a puppet theatre.

We struggled with all that gear because we wanted the occasion to be something really special for those children. Is it worth the effort? If the attitude of the children is anything to go by, it is. It is thrilling to receive rapt attention from a group of children, and to sense their excitement.

I'm convinced they're worth it.

And I think God thinks so too.

Owen Shelley